Vietnam Memoirs: Part 2

My Experiences as an Advisor with the Vietnamese Marine Corps

Don Bonsper

AroSage Publishing

ISBN-10: 1508649936

ISBN-13: 978-1508649939

Printed in the United States of America
First published July 2015

Excerpts from Selected Customer Reviews on Amazon.com about Vietnam Memoirs Part 1: My Experiences as a Marine Platoon Leader

This is a very good book that triumphs on the strength of its narrative of unfiltered observations: on war, on human nature, and especially on leadership. If you want to engage in a male fantasy of war, play a video game; if you want to know what it's really like, read this book. It is an easy book to read but a hard one to forget.

One of the best insights to knowing what these guys actually experienced in Vietnam. I really appreciated Mr. Bonsper's transparency in documenting this information that has always been a question mark in my mind.

"Vietnam Memoirs" gives us access to a world few will ever experience, and yet too many have endured. It takes us on Don Bonsper's journey from an idealistic young man eager to enter the fray to a seasoned veteran who understands all too well the realities of war. I think it should be proscribed reading for those studying this Era in American History.

Excellent! One of the most real stories you will read about Vietnam.

I like the writing style. It was not one of showing self but of selflessness. It was a refreshing breath of fresh air of a time of great sorrow and tragedy.

Bonsper tells the story of his time spent in Vietnam with honesty and candor. From the first time his company is sent out into the field to capture a hill (on his third day in Vietnam), to his eventual promotion and transfer to Saigon, the reader is fully engaged. From the horrors of extreme heat, flooding rain, mosquitoes, leeches, incoming mortars, and snipers; to the simple joys of receiving a letter from home or sleeping on a cot instead of on the ground, the reader is there by his side. Bonsper tells his story without apology for the jargon used by a Marine in the field, and the reader experiences all of the disappointment, anger, anguish, and frustration; as well as each moment of happiness, pride, and grace right along with him. It strikes home just how young these men were at the time they served, and the incredible issues they had to deal with – death, isolation from the world they knew, company politics, and an enemy that was virtually invisible. Through it all this incredible young man maintains his integrity, faith, and honor. This is truly a tale worth telling – and more importantly a tale every American who experienced this war only through images on their television should hear.

Riveting and fast paced but without any over-glorification of fighting a war. One would think all that the Vietnam conflict was about had already been written. One would be wrong. This is a very moving chronicle of what the majority of those who fought in Vietnam actually went through day to day. Can't wait for Part 2 to come out.

This memoir isn't filled with dramatic, Hollywood-style action. There is bravery but no Rambo. Bonsper gives us history at the micro level, an immersive read that conveys how it was and how it always seems to be in war for front-line infantry. The hurry-up-and wait, the unending tension and periodic terror broken by brief pleasures like a hot meal or the feel of a clean uniform, the zany operations ordered by commanders far enough to the rear to be out of touch.

If you have a son, grandson or nephew, consider this book as a gift. As I read it I thought of how inspiring this could be to young men (although I am female and enjoyed it very much!). There were many times while reading the book that I stopped and asked myself if I would have the strength, bravery, and courage to do what the men in the platoon were called upon to do. I think this book would be excellent for a high school history class, and students would have a great deal to reflect upon. It is inspiring to read of the courage of brave men and women like Colonel Bonsper who fought in Vietnam as the book provides a glimpse of the reality of the living hell of war and combat.

DEDICATION

To all the men and women who served in the Vietnam War with special recognition to the group of people who served as advisors with the Vietnamese Armed Forces. I know the life of an advisor with an elite unit of dedicated men, the Vietnamese Marine Corps, and want to thank them for their incredible contributions to the war effort and keeping me safe. They never wavered and remained committed to creating a free and independent South Vietnam. I also want to thank all the other advisors, especially those who worked with less trained and less disciplined units of the Vietnamese military. They are the real heroes of the advisor story. Finally, I want to acknowledge the families of the people who served. I have become more aware of the tremendous burden that is placed on those who are left behind and wait. With this in mind, I again dedicate this book to my soul mate for nearly 50 years, Pam. She was included in my first book as the one who taught me how to love. I include her here as the one who has taught me how to live life to a degree I could not do alone.

PROLOGUE

This is the second book in a two-part set that covers my year in Vietnam from June 1967, to June 1968. Part 1 was published in February 2015. It told the story of my time with Echo Company, Second Battalion, Ninth Marines of the United States Marine Corps. As a first lieutenant, I served as a platoon leader with the first platoon and then later as the company executive officer in northern I Corps. In late October 1967, I was simultaneously promoted to captain and reassigned to the Marine Advisory Unit in Saigon to serve as an advisor. Part 2 is the story of my time as an advisor with the Second Battalion, Vietnamese Marine Corps. I started my assignment as the assistant or junior advisor with an 800 man battalion of Vietnamese Marines. Three months into my time as an advisor, I went for 6 days of R&R with my wife, Pam, to Hawaii. I returned to Vietnam during the Tet Offensive. Later I was assigned as the senior advisor of that same battalion and became engaged in the largest battle of my time in Vietnam. I completed my one year tour of combat duty in June 1968.

CHARACTERS

Americans:

Colonel Richard Schaefer, USMC, Commanding Officer, Marine Advisory Unit in Saigon, Vietnam

Major Bob Corah, USMC, Senior Advisor to the Second Battalion, Vietnamese Marine Corps (VNMC)

Captain Don Bonsper, USMC, Assistant Advisor to Major Corah

Lieutenant Colonel Roger McKinley, USMC, Regimental/Task Force Advisor

Lieutenant Earle Hawks, USMC, Assistant Advisor to Captain Bonsper

Major Boyce Monroe, USMC, Replacement for Captain Bonsper as Senior Advisor

Captain Neal Andrews, USMC, Administrative Officer, Marine Advisory Unit

Major Jim Bennett, USMC, Artillery Advisor, VNMC

Lieutenant Commander Tom "Doc" Anderson, US Navy, Medical Advisor

Vietnamese:

.

Major Binh, Commanding Officer, Second Battalion, VNMC

Captain Nhung, Executive Officer, Second Battalion, VNMC

Captain Day, Commanding Officer of a separate company of a sister battalion, VNMC

Lieutenant Lanh, Commanding Officer, 2nd Company, VNMC

Private Trung, Radio Carrier, VNMC

Private Phuc, Cowboy or Batman, VNMC

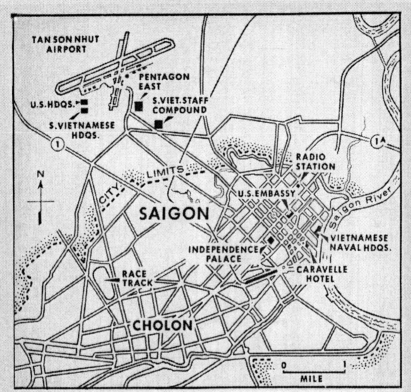

TAN SON NHUT
AIRPORT

PENTAGON
EAST

U.S. HDQS.

S.VIET.STAFF
COMPOUND

S.VIETNAMESE
HDQS.

1

RADIO
STATION

1 A

CITY LIMITS

N

U.S. EMBASSY

SAIGON

Saigon River

VIETNAMESE
NAVAL HDQS.

INDEPENDENCE
PALACE

RACE
TRACK

CARAVELLE
HOTEL

CHOLON

0   1
MILE

NXP060107-6/1/68-SAIGON: Allied forces 6/1 battled house-to-house again at
least 1,000 Viet Cong staging their 3rd invasion of Saigon in 5 months. Fighting
mushroomed into major combat with the Viet Cong entrenched in two sectors, one
a 10-block area in the heavily Chinese Cholon area.   UPI TELEPHOTO   ds

CHAPTER 1

NEW ARRIVAL

My Zodiac Seawolf wristwatch and I arrived in Saigon after five wonderful days in Okinawa. I had left Echo Company, Second Battalion, Ninth Marines at the end of October 1967, and taken a short detour through Okinawa to Saigon and my new assignment. I don't remember who suggested going through Okinawa but it turned out to be a great idea. When I had originally traveled to Vietnam in June 1967, I had left a B-4 luggage bag in Okinawa with uniform items and other things I would not need in country. By taking the little detour I was able to recover my bag from a large warehouse that was full of personal effects of the people serving in Vietnam. Also I was able to spend a few days of normal human living. I visited the family of a friend from The Basic School (TBS) and got a tour of the island which allowed me to see part of Okinawa's history from World War II. I slept in a bed, visited the officers' club and ate good food. Now as I arrived in Saigon I was somewhat refreshed although a little apprehensive. I was met by one of the administrative staff of the Marine Advisory Unit (MAU). I got my bag from the plane and was soon in a jeep heading for the unit's office in Saigon.

All of a sudden my apprehension increased; I was very nervous and unsure of myself. What was this advisor business going to be like? Just when I had been confident about what was expected of me as a platoon leader and company executive officer (XO), I had been plucked from the Second Battalion, Ninth Marines and sent to be an advisor. Now I would be starting all over again. As I rode along in the jeep my mind jumped back to my arrival in Vietnam nearly five months earlier and began analyzing what had happened to me, looking for lessons that could help me now.

I had been well prepared when I landed in Vietnam the first time in June 1967. The 21 weeks of basic officer training at Basic School in Quantico, Virginia had provided me with the necessary technical and tactical skills to arrive and immediately go into combat as a platoon leader. I was familiar with the weapons of the platoon and knew how to employ them. I was proud of my ability to read a map and use a compass. Land navigation was something that was critical in Vietnam and I was ready for it. There was also my physical condition to consider; I had been physically fit at TBS but all of us were. Almost five months had passed from the time I had graduated from TBS until my actual arrival in Vietnam. During that time I had worked hard to keep myself in good physical condition, expecting the demands of war to require all of my physical strength.

TBS had also taught me how to prepare and eat combat rations (C-rats or MCIs – meal combat individual). This was a small accomplishment while at Quantico but it was a giant advantage when I first joined my platoon. That first night I had been asked what meals I wanted for the operation at Hill 179. Being in the know about the twelve meals in the large box gave me a sense of confidence that I really needed. Then there were the men of the platoon. TBS had taught us about the platoon sergeant and the other key members such as the guide and radio operator. We had talked about the proper relationships that should exist in the platoon and how a platoon leader could help establish and maintain them.

My preparation for the war went beyond the lessons of Quantico. Politically I was supportive of the war. I believed the United States was doing the right thing to be in Vietnam. As a Marine I felt it was my duty to be there, to defend the U.S. and its interests. But beyond that, I wanted to be there to prove myself. I wanted to know if I was brave, if I was a man. Vietnam was where the action was and I wanted my share. The fact that I had to leave my new bride of 9 months was too bad. She had to accept my departure because I was a Marine and had a job to do.

It's funny how fast everything changed. Yes, I had been well prepared by TBS but I wasn't prepared for so much of what I found. My physical condition on arrival was not good enough for the heat and humidity of Vietnam, especially under the intense pressure of combat. Even though I could navigate all over Quantico, I found the navigation in Vietnam to be very difficult. The Government Issue compass was not easy to use and the maps were old. I should have bought a better compass before coming to Vietnam. I didn't correct that deficiency until I became an advisor.

My excitement about being in a war disappeared within minutes of my being pinned down on Hill 179. The war became too real as the first rounds cracked over my head. Did I think this was going to be like a football game, a contest, something I would play in and help my team win? That after I had added my part to the big game I could go home as one of the winners? That's how I thought before arriving in country. I would do my part and everything would be good. I was so wrong! I quickly learned that war is miserable, lousy, and certainly not just a game. I wasn't prepared for the elusiveness and competence of the enemy. Hill 179 was my first opportunity to feel the frustration of not seeing or finding the enemy during a firefight. That day the North Vietnamese Army (NVA) regulars allowed the lead elements of our company to get very close to their position before they opened fire. They did not shoot to kill but rather only to wound two or three people who then called out for medical help by yelling, "Corpsman, I'm hit." As expected, the corpsman raced forward to provide help and was promptly shot and killed. The other men were eventually killed or died as well. At the end of a long day of lying in the sun we finally reached the top of the hill, after a heavy air strike by our aircraft. We found our dead Marines and body parts of three 3 NVA soldiers. A month later, when we were ambushed coming out of the demilitarized zone (DMZ) it was even worse. This time the enemy waited for us to start moving down a narrow road before detonating a booby trap at the front of our column. As soon as the explosive detonated, the enemy mortar crews used that as their signal to start firing. We spent the entire day fighting our way back down that road. There were so many examples of our getting shot at and of even being engaged in tough firefights only to find no enemy dead when the fight was over. These experiences would play an important role in my future engagements as an advisor especially as I would become almost obsessed with finding bodies after a battle.

Initially I carried only a pistol as my personal weapon. After my introduction to combat with the fight on Hill 179, the pistol didn't seem like it was enough so I decided to carry something more. I wasn't interested in being able to shoot long distances but preferred to have something that would help me at close quarters. So I chose a 16 gauge pump action shotgun. After Hill 179 we had returned to Cam Lo for a couple of weeks. During that time we had patrolled every day to the west and south. It took about a half dozen patrols before I decided to "retire the shotgun." It was too heavy and interfered with my map reading and using the radio. I needed both hands to do my job and the shotgun got in the way. I spent the rest of my tour carrying only a pistol. When we came out of the DMZ and were ambushed I picked up an M-16 from a wounded Marine but only because of the situation. I felt that a pistol was enough under most circumstances. When it wasn't, there were always rifles available.

I learned some other lessons during my time as a platoon leader. One of the platoon sergeants from another platoon didn't wear socks or underwear. He said the socks prevented his feet from drying out after walking through the wet conditions of the terrain around rice paddies and the underwear caused rashes on the inside of his legs. I tried his method and found it to work. It took a few days for my feet to toughen up but then they were fine. He also only wore a skivvy shirt (T-shirt) under his flak jacket. He carried the utility blouse in his pack where it had a better chance of staying dry from rain or sweat. That way there was something drier to put on at night. I also followed his lead in this area. The long-sleeved blouse was relatively warm, dry, and a key weapon against the mosquitoes. However, the price I paid for carrying the utility blouse in my pack was constant cuts, scratches, and frequent infections on my arms.

As a platoon leader I had become close to my men. To me they were human beings and fellow Marines who were in the same tough situation as I was. TBS had been clear in its teaching about the proper relationships between the platoon leader and his men. But I chose to give the men nicknames or to use their first names. They called me lieutenant and I called them Sergeant "Mac", "Rudy", "Buck" and so on. They responded with a fierce loyalty that made them dependable and trustworthy. My company commander said that I was too familiar with my men. He later wrote the same thing on my fitness report. I had a hard time letting go of his criticism and find myself still harboring resentment for his comments. The ironic reality was that whenever he had a mission for one platoon, he sent mine. We were usually on the point when the company moved together. I may have been too familiar with my men but we always performed well as a unit and were asked to do more than our share of the workload.

There were at least two things I would do differently if I could do them again. I would make more use of supporting arms, especially artillery, to prep an objective before trying to take it. I would also put an external speaker on my radio. This was another lesson I would learn as an advisor. The external speaker would allow me to hear radio traffic as it occurred, thus eliminating the need for the radio operator to repeat everything. This would have saved valuable time during firefights and when we were pinned down by the enemy.

Finally, I had my feelings. My feelings about the dirty, inhuman aspects of war never went away. The Marine who lost his eye while I was checking the listening post, the lieutenant who was bayoneted in the groin and throat while being bound hand and foot, and the long line of bulging, rubber, body bags after we were ambushed coming out of the DMZ all convinced me that war should be avoided whenever possible. I now believe if a country must fight, then it should fight. It shouldn't pretend war is a game. You don't play wars; you fight them. A war must be executed with total dedication and intent to beat the enemy. Sadly, it seemed Vietnam wasn't fought that way. As I looked back on my time in the platoon, I now felt that we had thought too much about survival. We could have been more aggressive in our looking for the enemy. At the platoon level we had been extremely busy, almost too much so. We were caught up in numbers of patrols and other statistics without paying attention to the effectiveness of what we did. I remembered going from assignment to assignment, location to location, with no time to reflect or evaluate what had happened. I wondered if it would ever be possible to win the war.

My other feelings were those of loneliness. I had no idea how much I would miss my wife. I felt physical pain when I thought about being separated from her. This was one part of the war for which I was totally unprepared. But because of how I felt, I was able to understand the feelings of my married men and even the single Marines who missed members of their families. I should add that the feelings of loneliness were not confined to my time in Vietnam. After Vietnam there would be other long separations, this time leaving children behind with the wife. The separations never got easier but at least I knew what I was in for. The intensity of my feelings during that first separation in Vietnam was truly a surprise.

So now I had landed in Saigon and would start a new job as an advisor with the Vietnamese Marine Corps (VNMC). TBS had prepared me well for the position of platoon leader. My time as a platoon leader had forced me to adjust to the pressures of combat. I had learned some lessons that I would apply as an advisor. Some of my insecurity slipped away as I thought back on my time with the platoon. At least I had broken the jinx of the string of first platoon leaders being killed or wounded. I had seen my close calls but had been lucky enough to escape being wounded, injured or killed. I felt that now I was ready to take on the new challenge of working as an advisor with the Vietnamese Marines. I knew they were patterned after the US Marines and were considered one of the elite units of the Vietnamese Armed Forces. I looked forward to working with them as they struggled to save their country.

CHAPTER 2

ADVISOR AT LAST

As we headed toward Saigon in the jeep, I looked around at this new part of the war. Here was a large city with people, cars, buses, bicycles, scooters and large buildings. Everything was moving at a fast pace with plenty of noise from horns and people. My first reaction was to ask where the war was. This was so different from what I had seen up north in I Corps. There we saw very few people. The towns of Cam Lo and Dong Ha had small numbers of people living in them, but out in the field, we seldom saw anyone. When we did, we always stopped and asked questions about the Vietcong, but they just looked at us like we were from another planet. While at TBS I had taken a language aptitude test and scored pretty high. As a result, after graduation I had gone to eleven weeks of Vietnamese language training at the Defense Language Institute in Monterey, California before coming to Vietnam. The purpose of the training was to give me a limited capability to ask basic questions of the local people while I was operating at the platoon level. The school had been intense with 6 hours of language training a day plus long homework assignments at night. As a result I arrived in Vietnam with a reasonable capacity for basic conversation. The problem was I hadn't had enough opportunity to actually ask questions or to try to converse with the Vietnamese population. As I looked at the activity on the streets of Saigon, I suspected that I would have to re-learn everything I had studied about the Vietnamese language.

The fact that I had attended the language school was the reason I was now being assigned as an advisor. The Marine Advisory Unit (MAU) had suffered excessive losses from sickness and combat wounds. As a quick solution to the problem, the personnel system had looked at the Marines already in Vietnam who might be qualified to join the MAU. My language training at DLI put my name on the list. The additional facts that I had just been promoted to captain and had almost than five months in country as a platoon leader also helped me receive the assignment. Of course no one asked me about leaving E Company, Second Battalion, Ninth Marines. It was just part of the military world. There was a need for another advisor in the MAU and the system looked for the quickest and easiest solution to the problem. My name popped up and now I was joining a new unit and about to work in a completely new environment.

I was driven to the Splendid (pronounced splen-deed as if in French) Bachelor Officers' Quarters (BOQ) where I received a room. There were a number of different hotels in Saigon that were being used as BOQs for the international officers serving in the Military Assistance Command Vietnam (MACV). All officers serving with the MAU were billeted at the Splendid. I wanted to think that this

11

would be my new home but I was afraid to let myself get too excited. That was smart because I was quickly told that this was where I would sleep if I was in Saigon for any reason and where I could leave the gear I wouldn't be taking to the field. Yes, it was my room and would remain so until I left Vietnam, but my military assignment would not be in Saigon. It would be with an operating battalion and yes, I would be going back to the field and soon.

The next day I was introduced to Colonel Richard Schaefer, the commanding officer of the MAU and to the administrative staff. Everyone was friendly and appeared glad to have me in the unit. My experience as a platoon leader with the US Marines up north was viewed as a real plus. The dirty captain's bars I had received at the ad hoc promotion ceremony at Camp Carroll gave me an experienced look that I didn't feel. After a short tour of the Saigon offices and a quick briefing about the organization and mission of the MAU, I was off to a tailor to get measured for my jungle utilities. I had to buy two sets of utilities and a beret. The tiger stripe camouflage utilities were made of Vietnamese Marine Corps material and had the appropriate patches sewn on. My new unit would be the Second Battalion, Vietnamese Marine Corps. They were called "Trau Dien" which meant crazy water buffalo. A patch was sewn on my shoulder indicating the unit. Somehow I felt being a crazy water buffalo was just right for me.

The first two days in Saigon passed quickly. I can't remember whether I got the uniforms in the afternoon of the first day or went back the next day. I do remember that everything felt rushed and in a hurry. In addition to getting the proper uniforms I also remember going to a shop to get a hammock. I learned that the Vietnamese officers slept in hammocks whenever possible while operating in the field. I bought one of lightweight nylon that was sized to my 6 feet height and 175 pound weight. I had never spent much time in a hammock so was a little apprehensive about what it would be like to sleep in one. I knew it would require trees and space which had not been plentiful during my time in I Corps with the platoon. There was certainly an appeal to sleeping off the ground to get out of the bugs and water.

The administrative section under the leadership of Captain Neal Andrews was anxious to get me to my new unit where I would be the assistant advisor. So after no more than two nights in my BOQ bed with wonderful sheets and a pillow, I was driven north of Saigon to join the Second Battalion.

I met my American senior advisor, Major Bob Corah, met the Vietnamese officers of the battalion, and was assigned a "batman" or "cowboy" to carry my pack in the field. This was a surprise and something new. I had always carried my gear with the US Marines and felt uncomfortable having someone else carry my stuff. But this was the culture and custom within the VNMC. I also had a radio carrier. His job was to carry the radio so I could communicate with

Major Corah and other US units while engaged in an operation via our own radio frequency. He did not talk on the radio and was forced to stay close to me so I could use the handset. An external speaker mounted on the radio allowed me to listen to radio traffic without having to hold the handset. When it was necessary for me to talk I would get the handset from the radio carrier. This was a major improvement from my time as a platoon leader. There were only two Americans with each VNMC battalion, the senior advisor and the assistant. This meant two Americans and more than 800 Vietnamese Marines. Major Corah had been with the battalion about seven months so we would have about five months together before he would rotate back to the United States. It was unclear what would happen to me when he left. Would I stay with the battalion or would I be moved to a staff position? All of the senior advisors were majors and I would still be a captain. Time would tell.

We stayed in a battalion area north of Saigon for a few days. The pace was very different from that of the platoon. We were in a secure area which was almost like being in the rear. There were no patrols, operations, or field requirements. There was a US Air Force (USAF) base near our location which had an officers' club and swimming pool. I managed to get over there a couple of times but really felt guilty doing it. I always found myself thinking about the U.S. Marines up north, and the conditions under which they were living. How could I enjoy lounging around a swimming pool, reading a book, and drinking a cold beer when Rudy, Mac and the others were walking all over I Corps looking for the enemy?

I found that the Vietnamese officers all spoke English. There was no need for me to know Vietnamese in order to communicate with my counterpart or the other officers. The language training was valuable, however, when I had to talk with my batman, Private Phuc, radio carrier, Private Trung, or the other enlisted men of the unit. Both Major Corah and I ate with our counterparts. The battalion was commanded by Major Binh who had been fighting the Vietcong for years. My counterpart was Captain Nhung who prided himself on his strength and toughness. He too had been engaged in combat operations for years and proved to be an exceptional tactician. We would never become good friends even though we faced the horrors of war together. I always felt that he resented my presence in his country. Maybe we were too much alike in terms of our wanting to feel in control of any situation. We would grow to a mutually accepted condition of respect which allowed us to work together.

I would come to thoroughly enjoy the Vietnamese food but would always be on the lookout for American food or c-rations to supplement the rice, greens, chicken, duck, and pork that we ate in the battalion. One of my strongest memories of the first few days in the battalion position was the water supply. There was a large stream running behind the battalion Command Post (CP) building. I went out to the stream to bathe and was surprised to find how much

15

activity was taking place along both its banks. There were children splashing and playing in the dirty brown water. Upstream I could see women washing their clothes. Along the near bank I saw the battalion commander's cook washing the dishes we had used for the noon meal. I stepped into the water and started to wade out toward the middle when I saw human feces float by. It was then that I noticed two or three toilets built out over the water. There was an elevated walkway to get out to the toilets. A person could walk out, do their business with everything dropping into the stream and then walk back. I moved back to the stream's bank and again surveyed the activity that was taking place. It seemed that the small river was providing water for almost everything. I walked back to the battalion CP, found a five gallon can of clean water and took my bath by using my helmet.

These early days of no tactical concerns or requirements were actually a blessing. The quiet, peaceful time gave me a chance to feel comfortable in my new environment with the new language and new culture. One evening, the battalion had a large dinner for all of the officers. We had a long table with people seated down both sides. I don't remember what we had to eat but I know it was good. What I do remember is there was a small glass for each of us which had some kind of local whiskey. As the dinner started I learned a new game which was a custom within the battalion and possibly throughout all Vietnamese military units.

One of the officers, Lieutenant Trang, across from me lifted his glass and then drank down the whiskey. He passed his glass to me with a knowing grin on his face. I was confused. I wasn't sure what it meant or what I was supposed to do. I asked Major Corah and he smiled as he allowed one of the other Vietnamese officers to explain the rules. Captain Phuong explained, "When someone finishes his glass and passes it to another person, the second person is obligated to first drink down his own glass and then refill the glass of the first person. So, Dai uy (captain) Don, it is your turn to drink up and then serve Lieutenant Trang."

As instructed I drank my glass of whiskey and then refilled his glass. He in turn refilled my glass. Now we were all back where we started. The conversation started again and everything returned to normal for a few moments. Then a second officer finished his glass, put a smile on his face and passed it to me to refill. This meant I had to finish my glass again before I could refill his glass. It didn't take long for me to realize I was being ambushed by the larger force of officers. Over the next 30 minutes or so they would approach me one at a time and finish their glasses. They were many and I was one. They were each consuming one glass and I was consuming many. Slowly I became totally intoxicated. At one point I stood up and made a moving speech in Vietnamese about how happy I was to be there with them, to be an advisor and to help bring the war to a successful conclusion. I must have been pretty entertaining since everyone smiled and cheered me on. I felt like I was fluent in the language. At some point the evening ended. All I remember is that I was unable to get back to my sleeping area and just slept outside on the ground at the base of the flagpole. The morning hangover was brutal. It took most of the day to just start functioning without nausea and pain. Major Corah said I had been a good sport and had passed my first test in terms of being accepted. That made me happy to know there was some reward for the total devastation I felt. I promptly made a silent vow to never drink again.

Within another day or so we were off to the field on our first operation. As I had been told, I did not carry a pack. I wore my web gear with a pistol, canteens, knife and so on, but my poncho, poncho liner, hammock, and food were carried in the pack of Private Phuc. He seemed totally comfortable with the extra weight since he was also carrying all of his personal equipment. I later learned that the position of batman or cowboy with the American advisors was considered to be good duty. Phuc certainly looked like he was happy with his assignment.

Tactically the battalion operated very well. We moved on a dual axis concept. Two rifle companies and the headquarters company moved with the battalion commander while the other two rifle companies moved with the battalion executive officer. Major Corah as the senior advisor was with the Commanding Officer (CO), Major Binh, and as the assistant advisor I was with the Executive Officer

(XO), Captain Nhung. Major Corah and I could talk to each other on our advisor radio frequency. Our call signs were Leatherneck 2 and Leatherneck 2 Alpha. The 2 corresponded to the number of the Vietnamese Marine battalion. The VNMC had 6 battalions and each battalion had two US Marine advisors. All of us would be on the same radio frequency if operating together. The call sign numbers let us know who was in the area and what they were doing. We used the same radio frequency when working with supporting units from the US Army and Air Force. The radio turned out to be a most important lifeline among the advisors. There would be times when Major Corah and I wouldn't be together for days at a time. Since our Vietnamese counterparts didn't spend a lot of time keeping us informed, the senior advisor and I talked a lot on the radio about what was going on.

At night the battalion would set in either as a single battalion or as two separate units. We slept in hammocks with our poncho liners acting as blankets. The poncho was strung a couple of feet above the hammock to keep off the dew and the rain. We slept with the radios on, the external speakers off, and the handsets near our heads as close to one ear as possible. There was no one monitoring our radio frequency other than ourselves. It was amazing how quickly we could respond to radio traffic from a deep sleep.

Our first operation started slowly. I remember thinking back to Hill 179 and my first operation with the US Marines. It had been an eye opener in so many ways. Now I was off on my first operation as an advisor. Of course I really wasn't an advisor about anything, at least not yet. No one had asked me what we should do, how we should do it, where we should patrol etc. My job was to stay close to the XO and be ready to provide support as needed. I was actually glad no one looked to me for guidance on how to fight the war. The VNMC officers had been fighting the Vietcong (VC) and North Vietnamese Army (NVA) for years. I believed they knew what they were doing and was prepared to do my best to help when asked. I also realized my life was in their hands.

We walked for the first day and a half with no sign of the enemy, working our way carefully through heavily wooded and vegetated terrain. Then almost without warning there was heavy fire to the front of the battalion. I was with the XO when the firefight started. We were following behind elements of the lead company. I wanted to dive for cover when I noticed that he was still standing a few meters in front of me talking on his radio. He acted as though he were having a casual conversation with a close friend. At first the incoming small arms fire was not really close to us but it was coming in our direction. I could hear the tell tale cracks as the rounds passed high over our heads. Still talking on the radio, Captain Nhung looked at me to see my reaction. There was a small smile at the corners of his mouth. Our eyes locked and we just stood there. Did I see a little twinkle in his eyes? At first I was confused as to why he wasn't seeking cover but then realized that we were now playing some kind of a macho game. Suddenly, the incoming rounds got very close to us, cracking much louder over our heads. Captain Nhung looked at me and seemed to say that I had passed yet another test. He then moved directly behind a large tree while continuing to direct the lead troops via the radio. I followed his lead and moved close to the same tree, trying not to appear in too much of a hurry even though my stomach was turning cartwheels. All of this had taken only a couple of minutes. The shooting suddenly stopped and we were up and moving forward. Within minutes we crossed a deep trench line which connected a series of well constructed bunkers with overhead cover of large logs and dirt.

After we passed the trench line I could see we had entered a large enemy base camp. We found a large amount of rice and evidence that the camp had recently been occupied. The lead elements of our battalion had surprised a small group of enemy who apparently were guarding the base camp. Our lead elements had attacked and moved forward so quickly that the enemy had simply turned and run into the woods. We only took two wounded casualties and did not recover any enemy bodies. I had been impressed with the aggressive reaction of the Vietnamese Marines. They had simply moved so fast and so aggressively that the enemy had no time to mount any kind of a defense. This was my first exposure to the tactical proficiency of the VNMC. Again I compared this first encounter with the enemy as an advisor to my first operation with my platoon five months earlier. Then, we had been pinned down for hours by a small enemy force. This time was different. The experience of the Vietnamese Marine lead elements caused them to move rapidly against the enemy position. They reached the trench line so quickly that the enemy had no choice but to retreat. I suddenly felt that I was with a group of people who knew how to fight this war. It was a good feeling. The good combat reputation of the "crazy water buffalo" was well deserved.

We stopped and thoroughly searched the base camp. It was much larger and more intricate than it had first appeared. The bunkers and fighting positions were well made and obviously in usable condition. A series of well-maintained trenches connected the bunkers, most of which were constructed with substantial overhead cover and camouflage. I recalled the fighting holes we had dug on our little hill next to Con Thien. These bunkers were like hotels compared to our tiny holes. The heavy vegetation of the area made the base camp almost invisible from the air and definitely from the ground. If it had been defended, it would have been very difficult to attack and control. We had stumbled into the base camp by surprise with the added benefit that it was nearly empty except for the small guard force.

Now that we had control of the base camp, a decision was made by higher headquarters to destroy the bunkers with explosives. They were too useful to the enemy to just walk away and leave everything in working condition. Major Corah called on the radio to let me know that explosives and supporting devices to destroy the bunkers would be flown in by a U.S. Army helicopter. Since it was my half of the battalion that had found and taken the base camp, we were the ones that would destroy the bunkers. Somehow the responsibility for rigging the charges to blow up the bunkers fell on my shoulders. As part of my officer training at TBS I had worked with fuses, blasting caps, C-4 explosive, and detonating cord but had never expected to have to use the materials in a massive destruction project. The Vietnamese officers seemed totally content for me to take charge of the project. Could this be another one of their tests? I was beginning to wonder if they really wanted me as their advisor.

When the helicopter arrived, I sorted out the C-4 plastic explosive and supporting devices and tried to decide the best way to proceed. It was going to be a time consuming effort and it was going to be dangerous. The last thing I wanted to do was hurry and make a mistake. Once I got started the TBS instruction and training came back to me. In the beginning I wasn't sure how much explosive to use on the bunkers. As it turned out, I used too much on the first bunker which caused big chunks of debris to fly into the air. I had made sure that everyone was well back from the bunker so no one got hurt, but the stuff was landing too close; the Vietnamese officers looked at me like I was trying to get back at them for their drinking game.

I knew I had to reduce the amount of explosive for the next bunker. I remembered the casualties I had taken in the platoon on Hill 179 from the debris caused by the air strikes so I quickly reduced the C-4 to the right amount, enough to destroy the bunker but not too much to be a threat to the rest of us. I think there were 50-60 bunkers in total. It was going to take too long if I destroyed one bunker at a time so I looked for opportunities to build a daisy chain, a way to connect the bunkers, so I could do more than one at a time. This involved one fuse to set off the first string of detonating cord which set off the blasting cap in the first block of C-4, which was connected by detonating cord to the next block of C-4 at the next bunker and so on. The bunkers had to be close enough to make this multiple approach feasible both in terms of destroying the bunkers and safety for me and the Marines. At one point I used a daisy chain of explosives to blow up 7 bunkers at the same time. I honestly felt it was an almost perfect setup. The work went quickly and I had a couple of officers who helped me with stringing the detonating cord. At the end of the project I was pleased with how it had gone. This was another example of how well TBS had actually prepared me for what I might have to do in combat. This would be the one and only time I would have to work with explosives.

When the bunkers had been destroyed, we were again on the move. The rest of that day passed with no more enemy contact. We continued to move the following day but saw no enemy. In late morning we were told to change our direction and to move toward a U.S. Army battalion that had been in heavy contact with a large enemy force. Apparently they had taken significant casualties and still had some bodies that they couldn't recover. I wasn't sure what was waiting for us but I felt confident that my new unit would be up to the task.

As the orders were given to the company commanders to reflect the change in the battalion's plans I thought back on my first operation with the VNMC. They had moved well in the wooded terrain. Once in contact with the enemy they had responded with heavy fire and quick maneuver. I could see the advantages of fighting in familiar ground with an experienced group of people. When I remembered my time in the platoon I now appreciated just how hard it was. We faced constant turnover with people rotating in and out of the platoon. The terrain was unfamiliar to us and hard to learn in such a short time. And the enemy was different. He thought and lived differently from the way we thought and lived. In spite of these disadvantages the Marines of my platoon had done a super job. I prayed that they were ok. At the same time I was now grateful to be surrounded by these young, battle tested Vietnamese Marines. They had certainly demonstrated they were a force to be reckoned with.

The change of plans had been communicated to subordinate leaders and we were now on the move again. I considered my first

VNMC operation to be a successful one. During my first operation with my platoon at Hill 179, I had become accepted by my platoon as their platoon leader. They believed I was there to look out for their security and survival. This time I felt as though I had been accepted by my counterpart. Now we were off again to see what else the war had in store for us. As we moved out I wondered what we would find when we linked up with the Army battalion.

CHAPTER 3

CASUALTY RECOVERY

I had finished blowing up the bunkers of the enemy base camp the day before. My Vietnamese Marine battalion and I had continued to walk the rest of that day and part of the next when we received the orders to link up with a U.S. Army battalion that had been in heavy contact earlier in the day. We would spend almost the entire day walking in order to make contact with them before dark.

It was late in the afternoon when word was sent back to my position that our lead elements had made visual contact with the Army unit. I went forward to act as an interpreter and to help make liaison with the U.S. forces. What I found amazed me.

Yes, the Army unit had been in heavy contact early in the morning. They had been unable to advance because of the strong enemy defensive position and had to leave two or three of their men behind when they withdrew. I remembered my first day of combat on the side of Hill 179 and how helpless I felt. Now I was seeing another unit experiencing the same thing. The Army battalion had finally withdrawn to where we linked up with them and where all of us intended to spend the night. They had taken heavy casualties during the fight and still had the two or three missing men to account

27

for. They suspected that all missing troops were dead. Major Binh said that we would go back in to the area of the fight the following morning to recover their missing people. Meanwhile we had better coordinate our defensive position for the night. He also said his Vietnamese Marine battalion would take part of the defensive perimeter and the Army unit could have the remainder. We would form an oblong, circular formation and make positive physical contact at both ends where the two units would be side by side. We would look like two C's facing each other, with each side having its command elements inside their respective C.

When I coordinated with the Army unit I learned that there were three infantry companies in the field, each commanded by a captain. There was no battalion commanding officer, executive officer, or operations officer (S3) in the field with them. The three rifle companies were left on their own to pass the night. The CO and S-3 had been in a command and control (C&C) helicopter during the day, directing the battalion engagement from the air. When the fight ended they had returned to the rear with the choppers to spend the night and would be back in the morning. This was a shock to me. I couldn't imagine having almost the entire battalion in the field without the CO being there also. I could see the benefits of directing the battalion from the air when the conditions were right, but at the end of the day I would have expected the CO to rejoin his troops on the ground. That was only my first surprise.

The Army companies had spent the day without their packs. They had worn their web gear with canteens, rifle magazines and first aid pouch during the day and had carried one c-ration meal. Late in the afternoon, their packs were flown in by chopper along with a hot meal. Just before dark more choppers returned and sprayed over the unit for mosquitoes. To me the presence of the choppers coming and going was an invitation for mortars. I had plenty of experience with the noise from tanks advertising our position. The choppers were even better in a negative way. They could be observed flying to the position, hovering over an area and then landing. The enemy was plenty smart to know what lucrative targets were being serviced by the helos. The landing and taking off of the helos gave the enemy a good idea of the location of the unit and the number of helos helped determine the size of the force. All of this spelled trouble to me.

In the morning the choppers returned again, this time to deliver a hot breakfast and to pick up the packs. I was told by one of the captains that the Army battalion had also eaten ice cream the night before. Again I was surprised with the enormous difference between the conditions of various units. When I was with my platoon we carried everything, all the time. We never got a hot meal in the field and were lucky when we got some cold fried chicken, clean uniforms, and apples. The Vietnamese were carrying everything as well. We were not dependent on outside daily resupply to bring us our packs or food. When we received the orders to change direction and proceed to meet the US Army battalion, we just walked in a different direction. Everything was already with us. We were capable of continuing to operate with what we had. Of course we required periodic resupply of ammunition and other supplies but it was not critical to get something every day, or as in this case to have the choppers visit twice a day.

When the confusion of the morning choppers had ended, the Vietnamese Marines moved into the area of the previous day's battle. As expected, the enemy had left and we had no further contact. This was typical of my experience up north. We could have a firefight during the day and into the early evening and then stop. In the morning the enemy was gone, leaving next to nothing behind on the battlefield. The Vietnamese Marines found the missing bodies of the Army troops, all dead. I remember one young soldier was lying on the ground with 12 or 13 empty rifle magazines around him. He had obviously fought to the very end. His body had not been disfigured in any way. His wallet and ID card were both lying beside his body as though the enemy had looked at them. I sensed that the VC had left this young man's body alone as a sign of respect for his bravery. How different the NVA regulars had been when they tortured the third platoon leader in my old company before killing him with bayonets.

The recovery of the dead bodies and the detailed checking of the area consumed most of the day. In late afternoon we received orders to spend another night near the Army unit and to resume our separate operations the following day. Just like the previous night, the choppers appeared to deliver the packs and hot meals for the three Army companies. I felt that this was really pressing our luck. We knew the enemy had been in the area the day before because of the heavy contact with the Army unit. The repeated visits of the helicopters told the enemy where we were and continued to give an indication of our size and importance. I felt we were inviting an attack, either indirect via mortars or a direct ground attack. The portion of the defensive perimeter assigned to our battalion went around the edge of a large clearing. Parts of the clearing were bordered by a deep treeline and moderate vegetation. I was close to the actual clearing but was in the edge of the treeline and therefore had good trees for my hammock. We had been in the position long enough for my radio carrier and batman to dig a large hole in case we were attacked by mortars. I was pleased with the trees for my hammock and looked forward to a good night of sleep but some little voice told me the fighting hole was the most important part of our current location. Again, I was not disappointed.

Later in the evening the enemy probed our defensive lines to draw fire. I didn't give it much thought at the time; I felt it was more harassment than a serious attempt to prepare for a ground attack. Early in the morning, I was awakened by the now too familiar sound --toonk...toonk...toonk -- of the VC mortar crew. Just like the crews up north, this one was so skilled it could get all of its rounds in the air before the first round landed. How many rounds? I always thought it was around 50. I am not sure why I arrived at this number but I think it was mostly because I started counting as the rounds impacted and usually got to some number between 40 and 60. This is not too scientific but it gave me a way to start to anticipate when an attack would end. Maybe this was the number of rounds they could get in the air and still have a little time before the first round impacted. This meant they could break down the mortar and start escaping to somewhere safe before we had a chance to determine the direction of the incoming. If they had changed their tactics to shoot 80% of their rounds and then wait two minutes to shoot the rest, they would have increased their chances of killing their enemy. After the initial lull in the attack we would have been up and moving around and therefore better targets for the last 20% of their inventory of rounds. No doubt this would have added to the risk of the mortar crew being detected or attacked by counter battery fire from our forces. That never happened during any mortar attack I experienced except for the attack when we left the DMZ in July 1967. That time the enemy was not being clever or smart. It was simply a function of how many rounds they could prepare and fire at a time. The initial volley lasted a minute. Then there was a lull in the mortars and we could get moving down the road away from the DMZ. The lull was not too long and soon we heard the sound of more rounds on the way. This went on during the next couple of hours before the day morphed into an exercise in moving a little to the south between attacks and in response to the ground attack that was mounted at the same time. In this case the enemy had no intention of running away. The mortar attacks were well planned and orchestrated to keep us confused and vulnerable. They had a large American unit within their range and they had no intention of just firing one volley of mortar rounds and leaving the battlefield. They wanted to keep us right where we were. They moved the mortar tubes in between volleys but that was so they could increase their likelihood of survival and to keep us unsure as to where they were.

But this morning, I screamed "incoming" as I heard the sound of the incoming rounds and looked for the relative safety of my fighting hole. For some unknown reason I was disoriented as I rolled out of my hammock. I first crawled in the direction of where I thought the hole was but no luck. No hole in that direction, only an open path to the clear area. I changed course and tried another direction but still couldn't find the hole. The mortar rounds were now landing but they weren't close to my location. Instead of just lying on the ground where I would have been relatively safe, I continued to crawl around like a broken windup toy looking for my hole throughout the entire attack. Just as the mortar rounds stopped landing, I finally found the hole. Trung and Phuc were safe in the hole with big smiles on their faces as though they were wondering why I had taken so long to arrive. I hoped they hadn't been watching my crawling efforts during the attack. Again I had been lucky. We had tempted fate and we got what we deserved. I am sure all of the Vietnamese officers and troops felt the same way I did. We had broadcast to the enemy world that we were a large enough force to require helicopters for support and would therefore be a great target. The fact that we were two different military units was not important to the enemy; the more of us the better in terms of a target.

The Trau Dien took no casualties from the attack with most of the mortar rounds falling within the part of the perimeter occupied by the Army troops. It made sense that the mortar crews would have concentrated on that part of the perimeter since that is where the helicopters landed and departed. Once again, I believed we had invited the mortars by staying in the same location for the extra day and by the multiple visits of the choppers. I appreciated the value of a hot meal but really questioned the need to have two hot meals every day. Again I remembered the long periods in the field with my platoon up north with no hot meals, the same filthy uniforms, and the total dependence on carrying what we needed. Operating without the weight and restrictions of a pack is smart. Given a choice, I would have preferred to move all day without a pack and to have it delivered to us at night. My experience up north had not included that option. We had carried what we needed. We did not have the helicopter support to bring out food and packs at the end of the day and to pick them up in the morning. We also never really knew for sure what would happen during the day. It would have been hard to plan the end of the day worrying about the packs etc. I think our way worked given the conditions we faced. The need to have my stuff close at hand has stuck with me to this very day. Many people think I'm crazy but I always travel by air with my luggage as carry-on. I am willing to drag my bag all over the airport and between departure gates just to know it is with me. I will wash my clothes in the sink of a hotel or airport. I will do without "extra" of almost anything just to ensure I am able to take it all with me all the time.

Still, the Army had the air assets and they were using them. Tactically, I felt the choppers had been the major cause of the mortar attack. Their coming and going had marked the combined location of our forces. The probing of the lines the night before had helped pinpoint that location. Logistically the choppers had served the needs of the Army battalion very well. I never saw the battalion CO spend any time with his unit in the field. The three company commanders, all captains, fended for themselves. They were just like me. We were all young officers doing the best we could. Lessons can be learned both by observing positive leadership and negative leadership. I hoped I would remember these lessons when I got my opportunity for battalion command.

With the morning mortar attack behind us we again were on the move. We continued to operate as a battalion through the rest of

December. We had a few minor contacts but nothing of significance. Christmas came, and with it, a truce. I was very skeptical about a truce but somehow it was honored by both sides. We went through the holiday with no enemy contact and a few opportunities to just slow down and relax. After Christmas and the ceasefire, we received orders to move to the Mekong River Delta area south of Saigon. This would give me a chance to see another combat zone or "Corps" of Vietnam. I had spent almost 5 months in I Corps with the U.S. Marines and now had almost two months in III Corps as an advisor. The movement at the end of December to the Delta would put me in IV Corps for the first time. I would not get a chance to operate in II Corps, the only other military combat zone of South Vietnam.

Before moving to the Delta, I had decided that I would go ahead and take my Rest and Relaxation (R&R) at the end of January. Each military person serving in Vietnam was authorized to take 6 days of R&R during the year long (Army) or 13 month (Marines) tour of duty. The government would provide air transportation to and from the R&R site but all other expenses were the responsibility of the individual. Many married military personnel went to Hawaii to meet their wives. Many single soldiers and Marines went to other locations in the geographic area, places like Taipei, Bangkok, Manila, and Hong Kong. There would be another truce during the period of Tet, the Vietnamese Lunar New Year, at the end of January which would mean that I probably wouldn't miss anything of operational importance while I was gone. It would also reduce the demand on the advisor who would have to take my place while I was in Hawaii with Pam.

We moved from our position north of Saigon to our new operating area in the Delta by trucks and jeeps. It was an all-day road movement that was hard on my young body. I sat on an ammo can covered with a pillow between the driver and Major Corah in a jeep. I did not complain. It was nice to be with my senior advisor all day to talk, laugh, and think about the future.

After we arrived and got fully settled our operational tempo started to pick up. Our planned method of operation was to patrol by foot for 3-5 days and then move into a local village for a day or so to wait for our next orders. We were operating in the area of responsibility (AOR) of a Vietnamese Army Regiment (ARVN) but operated alone. Our intelligence about the enemy forces and their locations came from both Vietnamese and American sources. Our artillery support came from the Vietnamese Marine Artillery battery. Air support was provided by the U.S. Army and Air Force.

It was still early January when we were told we would be conducting a battalion-sized helicopter borne assault within a short period of time against a suspected enemy regiment. I found myself doubting that an enemy regiment or even a battalion could be moving around in the Delta without everyone knowing where they were. It seemed the mere size of such a force would make it next to impossible to conceal. I acknowledged the Delta was full of small waterways and canals that were difficult to see from the air, but a regiment or battalion? My previous experience said no way. This time the intelligence sources got it right and a large, determined enemy force was in fact right where they said it would be and it was waiting for us.

CHAPTER 4

ENEMY TRAPPED

Things happened fast once we learned about the presence of the suspected enemy force in our area of operations. We met in the evening of 8 January 1968, to plan the operation for the next day. There were the two advisors from my battalion plus representatives from the Army helicopter outfit that would be lifting us during the operation. We also had representatives from the US Air Force who would be available to help coordinate air support. Our battalion had set up its defensive position near a small village and we met in a local building. Our Vietnamese counterparts were there and were happy for us to take the lead. They asked questions about the planned operation and we served as their liaison and special language interpreters. They all spoke English but would turn to us to make sure they understood every nuance of what was being discussed. If there was any confusion they would ask us their questions. We knew what the questions really meant so we in turn would ask the same questions of our American counterparts but with the subtle emphasis to ensure we responded to the concerns of the VNMC. We talked about where we would be picked up, what time, the numbers of troops per chopper and so on. This operation was going to be a large assault with plenty of choppers. Frankly, I doubted that many helicopters would actually be made available for our use the next day. Like so many times before, I was basing my beliefs on my personal experience up north. Again I underestimated the assets that came with US Army support.

The latest intelligence now said the enemy was either a VC battalion or regiment and was believed to be located near the upside down "T" intersection of two large canals: one canal running north and south (up and down on the page) and stopping at a second canal running east and west (left and right on the page), thus the intersection. The enemy unit, whatever its size, was believed to be well armed with mortars and 50 caliber machine guns along with the small arms weapons of an infantry unit. Intelligence sources thought they moved by small dugout boats and canoes using the extensive network of canals of the Delta to travel large distances and were extremely mobile and able to appear in places where no one thought they could be. Later we would identify the actual unit we were chasing as the Viet Cong 261B Main Force Battalion.

The plan of operation called for us to land the entire battalion in two pieces. Half of the battalion would be lifted to a landing zone (LZ) east and south of the intersection along the east-west canal while the remaining half would be lifted to an LZ north and east of the intersection. The intersection of the two canals would be a key point in terms of the initial landings. I would be with the XO, Captain Nhung, and his half of the battalion on the south side and

Major Corah would be with Major Binh and the rest of the battalion on the north side. After landing, both halves would consolidate their positions and then first move toward each other into the thick treelines which grew along the banks of both canals but primarily the east-west canal. Once in the treelines the battalion would sweep west along the canal in the direction of the intersection. The northern half of the battalion (led by Major Corah and Major Binh) would have the north-south canal as a stopping point. The southern half of the battalion (led by Captain Nhung and me) would not be restricted in its movement to the west but would not want to initially pass the intersection point with the north-south canal.

Our pickup LZ early the following morning, 9 January, would be along a straight and narrow dirt road which was slightly elevated above the surrounding rice paddies. The choppers would land perpendicular to the direction of the road so it was critical we had all of our teams divided up and spread out when the choppers arrived. It would be very difficult and dangerous to move around the front or back of one helicopter to get to another without getting down off the road and then back up on the road. It would also slow everything down if people weren't in the right place to start with.

Morning arrived after a quiet night and we moved out to the LZ along the road and prepared for pickup. We were early as usual. The battalion was so disciplined in its execution of orders that it made sure no one could say the VNMC was not ready when the choppers arrived, especially when they were coming from US forces. There was a level of excitement or tension in the air that I hadn't really felt before. Somehow everyone knew this was going to be a special day with heavy enemy contact likely. While we waited along the road, looking and listening for any sign of the incoming aircraft, we established radio contact with the chopper pilots as they were en route to our position for pickup. They said the preparation of the LZs near the objective area was on schedule and that both LZs were hot, meaning they were already under fire. In this case the helicopter gunships prepping the LZ had taken 50 caliber fire from the treelines which indicated there was a good-sized unit in there; 50 caliber guns were big and heavy and went with big enemy forces. This should have triggered a bell in my head. Normally the enemy would not respond to the preparation fire at a possible LZ location. Maybe they thought the gunships were just flying around and shooting at random targets. I don't think so. Normally they would remain quiet. I think they were sending a message: "Don't come to this location because we are waiting for you." The presence of such a large weapon as a 50 cal supported the intelligence about an enemy force of battalion or regimental size. Landing in hot LZs was not good. It was one thing to land in a hot LZ as a surprise and then react and operate as the situation unfolded. In a way this was bad but maybe better than the alternative. In this case it was entirely different to be listening to a radio transmission about what was going on in the area you were headed for. Knowing ahead of time that the LZ was hot caused an observable increase in the tension level. Everyone looked serious and spent extra time checking their weapons and ammunition. Radio operators ensured their radios were working by running a few extra radio checks. Major Corah and I looked at each other and thought about what would actually happen when we landed and how the operation would go. Then as if there wasn't enough to think about, one of the young Vietnamese Marines carelessly tried to walk behind a helicopter that was sitting on the road. He walked down one side of the chopper and then turned to go behind it so he could get to the other side. He walked right into the tail rotor. He was immediately decapitated and killed. His body flew into the air in a mixture of blood and pieces. It was a good reminder of just how dangerous everything was in a combat zone. No one needed to see this tragedy at this critical moment of boarding. As I climbed into my helo, I had a strong feeling this was going to be a day to remember.

Our half of the battalion (the XO and two companies) was further divided into two helicopter lifts. One company would be carried in each lift. Once airborne, it wouldn't take long to arrive near the objective area. The XO and I were with the lead company. As usual I would be working with the XO who would have overall operational control of the two companies. The battalion commander and Major Corah would be with the other two rifle companies and the headquarters company. According to the operational plan our half would land on the south side of the objective and they would land on the north. Then depending on the situation we would move north to the treeline; they would move south to the treeline. It was important that we not shoot at each other. If the intelligence was good, we should encounter the enemy force in the treeline along the east-west canal. The intelligence said the force was close to the intersection but it was entirely likely they were spread out along the canal in the treeline, especially if the force was as large as we thought. We would need to make visual and radio contact between our two parts of the battalion and then start our sweeping of the treeline to the west toward the intersection. It made perfect sense that any enemy forces would be concealed in the treelines since the terrain away from the canals was open and full of dry rice paddies. It offered very little cover and concealment as we would soon find out.

As we came into the landing zone, the escort helicopter gunships really poured fire into the treelines. They used their machine guns and rockets and laid down a blistering amount of suppressive fire. It was hard to tell if and how much return fire they were receiving but for sure they were under fire. As a result the transport choppers carrying us did not land as close to the treeline as we had originally planned. This was a good thing. It is a good example of changing plans on the fly. The pilots knew the LZ was hot. They knew the closer they landed to the treeline the more risk they took for themselves and for their valuable cargo which included me. If they could get us safely on the ground without losing a chopper and still have us close enough to the original LZ then a change made sense. This meant our actual landing wasn't that bad in terms of incoming fire. We did not exit the choppers and face immediate heavy fire from the enemy. We were able to disembark from the choppers and move into a defensive position which gave us control of the LZ and then send our lead elements toward the treeline while we waited for the second lift with the rest of our force. The main issue for us was getting oriented to our location and accepting the fact that we would have to move a greater distance to get close to the enemy position. That was really my thinking as I left the chopper and observed the initial situation. That turned out to be a bad assumption. As I ran from my chopper I could hear the sounds of a serious fire fight between me and the treeline. Obviously the aggressive Marines of the lead element had headed to the treeline right after landing. My radio carrier and I followed Captain Nhung as we ran into a small gully that was parallel to the treeline. The XO was in radio communication with the lead elements who were in heavy enemy contact. I learned it was as I had originally thought. After landing they had quickly crossed the open rice paddy and gotten close to the treeline but could not push their way in. The enemy was dug in and returning heavy machine gun and small arms fire.

The XO looked at me with a "let's see what you can do" look and said, "Dai uy Bonsper, we need air support as quick as possible." It is important to understand that he was not operating on his own. He was in communication with Major Binh who had Major Corah at his side. The decision to start working the advisor network to get air support followed a strict chain of command. In some ways I was at the bottom of this most important chain. I would be the one to actually get and control the air support that other people wanted and badly needed and that other people told me to get. This would be the first time I had actually requested or controlled any kind of air support for the battalion. I told myself this was why I was here-- to help with the control of supporting arms. Blowing up some bunkers in an enemy base camp was a nice contribution to the overall effort but that was not why I was here nor was it a reason to justify my presence in this unit on this day. My value as an advisor was highest when the situation was at its worst. It seemed my day of reckoning had arrived.

I told Captain Nhung, "I will get the air support. What I will need are as many details as you can provide about the locations of our troops and the enemy. You can tell your men when to pop a smoke grenade to mark their positions." I got on the radio through the miraculous Leatherneck frequency – a radio frequency dedicated to the Marine advisors and their support -- and started to explain our situation and immediate need for air support. The response was beyond expectations. One minute I felt isolated and alone along the dike of a rice paddy. Gunfire was erupting in front of me and I knew we were in a bad place at a bad time. And then almost like I had moved to another place and time I was in radio contact with the first team of supporting aircraft. I can't remember what kind of aircraft showed up in response to my first request but I think they were F-4 Phantom jets.

"Leatherneck 2 Alpha this is Foxfire 47, I understand you have some issues on the ground."

I responded, "Foxfire 47, great to hear your voice. Yes, we are engaged with a dug-in enemy and are totally unable to advance." This was only the first communication from a large group of wonderful pilots that would provide support for the entire day. The pilots calmly checked into the communications net and asked for a description of the target and for instructions as to how they could help. I first gave the pilots a general idea of the action. They could easily see the firefight below them so the main concern was that they didn't hit any of our troops. There was no question about the two opposing forces being very close to each other. This demanded that the pilots have total confidence in where they fired their weapons which meant I had to give them precise information about the location of the friendly forces. Captain Nhung told me where his lead elements were and where the enemy was located. I talked to the aircraft, trying to describe the terrain and location of our troops as it had been described to me. But that wasn't good enough. I was just repeating what the XO told me and he was repeating what the lead company commander was telling him. I had to be able to see more of what I was trying to describe.

The gully was too deep for me to see well enough over the top to direct the airstrikes. I stood up and then crawled up the side of the gully so I could look over the edge of a small rim that ran along the gully. Private Trung was close beside me with his whip (long) antenna on the radio. He had to move with me because of the length of the cord on the radio handset. It wasn't long enough so I could move very far without forcing him to move with me. As I crawled up the side of the gully and carefully looked over the edge there was a sudden increase in the level of small arms fire in our direction. I could hear the loud crack of the bullets as they flew over our heads. They didn't seem to really be that close and I didn't think they were a real direct threat to Trung and me. Still I was smart enough to know they were coming our way. I knelt back down in the gully and noticed the sound of the rounds stopped. That seemed strange. I wondered why the intensity had slacked off. After a minute or so of deep thinking, I stood back up and slowly looked over the rim of the gully and again the rounds started flying over our heads. Again I slid back down into the gully and the rounds stopped. This was *really* strange. I thought to myself, *I'm a Fulbright Scholar, a Naval Academy graduate. I'm supposed to be smart. There has to be an explanation for this change in incoming fire.* I looked at Trung who had a confused expression on his face that I did not interpret

48

correctly. For some unknown reason I repeated the up and down movements three or four more times before I realized the enemy was in fact shooting at us and was using the whip antenna on the radio as a way to mark our location. They couldn't really see me as a target but they could see the antenna pop up when I stood up so they just directed their fire at the area close to the antenna. They knew the antenna represented someone important, a good target, and maybe one that was capable of doing them damage. I felt pretty stupid when it finally became clear to me. I looked at Trung and he had a small smirk on his face, almost like that sure took a long time for you to get the message. That was all the attention I needed to shift to the tape (short) antenna which was not visible to the enemy.

It turned out the air strikes were easier to control than I had expected. While a student at TBS we had learned the procedures to call in and control artillery fire, naval gunfire and close air support. There was a protocol to follow and a series of questions/answers that would define the target, locate friendly forces, provide routes in and out etc. But this was the real world and it was nasty. Time was critical and things were happening so fast. The pilots were incredibly experienced and knew what they were doing. Little did they know that I was an air support "rookie" and doing this for the first time. Rather than worry about proper radio procedures, the pilots talked to me like we were having a regular conversation at some sidewalk café and calmly asked me for a description of the target and its location. I did my best to follow proper radio procedure and tell them about the target. They did the rest. It was amazing that we were talking about "a group of banana trees" or the "thick brush east of the yellow smoke from a smoke grenade." The battalion would pop smoke from a smoke grenade to mark our positions, the pilots would identify the color of the smoke, and if all was well would deliver their ordnance. We never revealed the color of the smoke grenade ahead of time. We knew the enemy could listen to the radio transmissions and could also pop a smoke grenade. If we said we were going to use a particular color, the enemy could do the same to confuse the pilots. There were stories of friendly units telling the color ahead of time and then the pilot seeing multiple smoke grenades go off while the enemy pretended to be a friendly force.

When one flight of aircraft, usually two or three planes, had used up its ordnance and fuel it would leave the target area and be replaced by another. The deadly effects of the air strikes allowed the Vietnamese Marines to advance initially, but soon they were too close to the enemy and the day became another stalemate. We couldn't push through the enemy and they couldn't get away from us. It was like we were stuck together with glue. I felt worried but also excited that we had trapped a large enemy force that could not withdraw during daylight because that would cause them to be more visible from the air. For the moment, they were stuck where they were.

For the rest of the day I directed air strikes that bombarded the treeline. The VNMC remained in close proximity to the enemy and continued trying to advance. The sky was full of aircraft waiting to help us out. My radio frequently came to life: "Break, break. Leatherneck 2 Alpha this is Blackjack One Three. Can I give you a hand down there?" I had fixed wing jets or fast movers, helicopter gunships, A-1E Skyraider propeller driven slow movers, and airborne forward air controllers (FAC) in their little observation aircraft. It was a lifetime of directing air strikes all crowded into one long day. At times the flights of aircraft were stacked up three deep or better said three high. When there were multiple groups of aircraft circling high above our position while the lower level aircraft were actually conducting airstrikes, it was important to know the fuel levels and remaining time on station for those who were waiting. The airborne FAC was in contact with everyone, filling the role of orchestra leader with aircraft as instruments and firepower as music. I was focused on the attacking aircraft. Sometimes the FAC and I would have to interrupt the striking A-1Es or gunships in order to let the jets make their runs because their fuel was low. When they were finished, we could bring the longer duration A-1Es back on the target. I can't remember the radio call signs of all the different units that came to help during the day, but there were a whole bunch. Still with all of the well placed firepower, we couldn't move the enemy back and get into the treeline. I knew, however, that we had to be inflicting damage to his forces.

The second half of our battalion had landed on the north side of the canal but had been unable to advance to the south because of our firing in their direction. They spent almost the entire day just staying out of the way of our bullets. They were able to move west to the north-south canal. On our side of the canal, we had spent the day engaged in the most serious firefight I had seen in Vietnam. As the day was drawing to a close, the XO told me our half of the battalion was running low on ammunition. We had used up almost all of our smoke grenades while making sure the airstrike planes knew where we were. We were very low on M-16 rifle and M-60 machine gun ammo as well. In addition to the ammunition problem, we were essentially stuck in an open rice paddy and were very exposed. This made us vulnerable to a counterattack because of a lack of real cover. We had spent the day moving in small gullies and along rice paddy dikes, using them for as much protection as we could get. The lead elements were in heavier vegetation since they were closer to the treeline. For some reason I hadn't thought much about our exposed situation given my total preoccupation with the control of the air support. But now it was getting dark and the airplanes were gone. Suddenly I felt as though the momentum of the day was shifting to the enemy.

Since the actual firefight was really over and the shooting had stopped, the other half of our battalion was able to continue their movement to the south. I spoke to Captain Nhung about trying to trap the enemy where he was by making sure the escape routes along the two canals were blocked. For the first time, I strongly emphasized my opinion. "We have to do this," I said. I finally felt like an advisor. The XO agreed and we sent part of one of our companies to the west and then north to take up a position along the east-west canal to the west of the intersection. This would prevent the enemy getting away to the west along the east-west canal. The other half of the battalion moved west until they reached the north-south canal. This should prevent the enemy getting away by going north on that canal. That half of the battalion also had troops in the treeline to the east of the enemy position as did we. It seemed as though the enemy had no way to get out. I knew he was a master at moving along the canals in small, quiet boats and canoes but I was sure this time he was caught. Even though we wouldn't be able to do anything until morning, I felt as though we were in position to successfully end the battle with a new day. For once, I was totally confident that we had the enemy right where we wanted him. Then I remembered the shortage of ammunition and what might happen if the enemy decided to attack rather than try to get away.

The XO gave me a list of what the battalion needed. I called for a helicopter ammo resupply and the battalion prepared an LZ which provided as much protection for the chopper as possible. The LZ was on the south side of our position, away from the treeline with some of our forces between the LZ and the trees. But since we were essentially in an exposed, flat rice paddy the LZ was totally visible and vulnerable to enemy fire.

Shortly after dark, the helo pilot checked in, "Leatherneck 2 Alpha this is Valor 45 en-route to your position over."

I replied, "Valor 45, this is 2 Alpha. Good to hear your voice. We need your cargo. I will move out into the LZ with a flashlight to mark our position. Let me know when you see my light, over."

The helo was accompanied by two gunships that opened suppressive fire on the treeline. As the helo slowly came toward our position I moved out into our LZ with Private Trung and shined my flashlight directly at the approaching chopper. I was able to talk to the gunships and the resupply helo. The combination of my flashlight and the sound of the approaching helos caused the enemy to start shooting again.

The pilot reported, "Leatherneck 2 Alpha I am taking fire in and around my bird."

I knew there was a lot of enemy fire but it was hard for me to hear anything over the noise of the chopper. I was unaware of how much fire was directed at my location and how much was going at the chopper. I could see tracer rounds from the enemy heavy machine gun passing through the sky, mostly over the chopper, and I could hear cracks passing over my head. I naively believed it would be ok. The ammo resupply was so important I just focused on making it happen.

I responded, "Valor 45, you will be ok. I can see the tracer rounds and they are passing over the top of your chopper. Get down as low as you can and come on in."

I will never forget his response, "2 Alpha, I've got rounds going over, under, and through me. I'm not coming in any closer. We're pushing the ammo out the door."

I quickly replied, "Please don't push it out the door. If you do we'll never find the ammo in the dark. Please come back and give it another pass and let's see what happens. I'm sure we can complete the mission."

Too late! No luck. He said the ammo was out the door and someplace on the ground and he was returning to base. As he flew away with the gunships, I tried to understand the feelings of the helo pilot but it was hard. The events of the day had taken their toll on all of us and I was starting to worry about the ammunition. I was very selfish in putting the needs of the battalion first. I remembered when we had fought our way out of the DMZ in July with the platoon and a helicopter had been shot down. The loss of the helo that day did not affect me personally. Now it was personal and we needed the ammo. I later learned that one of the gunships had been hit during our failed resupply attempt. Obviously the enemy wasn't ready to quit. The resupply chopper had come and gone and the ammo had been dropped someplace out in the rice paddy. The dark green cans would have landed and sunk in the soft damp ground of the rice paddies. The XO coordinated an exhaustive search for the ammo as best as possible under the limited light and challenging tactical conditions but never found it. I returned to the Leatherneck radio frequency and asked for another resupply chopper. I explained what had happened with the first attempt and promised we would do better to keep the LZ clear of enemy fire the next time and to direct the chopper along a safer route in and out.

Later that night, well after dark, I received a radio call saying that another chopper would soon be approaching our position with the badly needed ammo resupply. This was good news. I had started to accept that we would pass the night with what we had in terms of ammo and smoke grenades. It was so quiet as we waited for the helo to check in on the radio. In some ways it was another beautiful night in Vietnam. The heat of the day was gone and the relative freshness of the night was a welcome relief. I often thought how sad it was that we could never really enjoy the beauty of anything around us. This included the rough terrain of northern I Corps, the wooded flatlands of III Corps, and the lush vegetation of the Mekong Delta and IV Corps with its rivers, canals, and rice paddies. Still waiting for the helo pilot to check in, the night suddenly came alive with the too familiar toonk--toonk--toonk sound of the Viet Cong mortars. Not again. My mind flashed back to my time with the platoon: getting mortared coming out of the DMZ in July, again south of the

DMZ in September, on the little hill west of Con Thien in early October. Then as an advisor there was the night after we had linked up with the three US Army companies in December. Now here they came when it had been the farthest thing from my mind. There was no place to get any real protection. There had been no chance to dig foxholes during the day plus we had no intention of spending the night in the rice paddy when the day started. So everyone just lay flat on the ground in the rice paddy, hugging the little dikes, looking for any kind of depression in the ground we could find and hoping for the best. The mortar rounds landed all around us. The XO's radio operator was lying next to me and was hit with shrapnel in the leg and side. He was one of a handful of Marines who had been wounded. Luck was with me again as I escaped untouched. No one had been killed but the new casualties added to our problems and complicated the logistics of our resupply. Now we had new casualties to evacuate in addition to still needing the ammo.

I was jerked back to reality when I heard on the radio, "Leatherneck 2 Alpha this is Smiley 17. I have some stuff I think you're looking for." This was great. This time I knew we had to get the resupply. Nothing could go wrong. We had to get the helo on the ground to get our ammo and we had to be able to load our casualties.

"Smiley 17 this is 2 Alpha. We had some problems with the last attempt at a resupply so we want to get it right this time. I want you to start your approach as far away as possible and as low as you can fly. Turn off your lights. Direct your escort gunships to fire on the treeline to your front and behind me. Look for my flashlight and use it for your heading. I will be standing in the LZ."

The pilot immediately replied, "Roger that 2 Alpha. When you say flashlight, exactly what do you mean?"

"Smiley 17, I mean a handheld, Government Issue, 2 D cell flashlight. I will be pointing the light directly at you as you come to our position. I will try to position the light to make it easy for you to see and will move the light lower as you get closer. Stay low and go as slow as you can. Touch down in front of me as close as you can. Trust me that the LZ is ok in terms of obstacles etc."

I'm glad he didn't laugh at my flashlight. He simply responded, "Sounds good 2 Alpha. I am on my way. Let's get this done."

As the resupply helicopter approached our location my loyal radio carrier and I did our best to provide a good source of light for the chopper. I had my back to the enemy position in the treeline which concealed most of my light source and also gave the helo the safest heading to approach our position. Of course the light from my flashlight was going away from me and illuminating some of the ground to my front but I hoped it would not be that visible to the enemy. Far out on the dark horizon I could hear what I believed was the chopper coming straight toward me.

I asked the pilot, "Smiley 17 I can see you approaching our

58

position. You look good. Keep it low and slow. Do you have my light?"

A few seconds later, he replied, "I have your light. I am as low as I can get and coming in slow. The grass is tickling the belly of my bird. Wiggle your light so I'll know it's you."

I stood steady with just a little movement of the flashlight.

He came back, "Got it. I'm coming in."

I had the radio in one hand and the flashlight in the other, doing my best to babble about how all was looking good to convince him that all was well and things were looking positive for a successful resupply. I couldn't hear anything above the noise of the helicopter plus the fire from the gunships so I wasn't sure if the enemy was shooting at us or not. I was so intent on talking to the resupply pilot and making sure the gunships were on target with their suppressive fires that I just lost awareness of everything around me except for this one helo bringing our badly needed ammo. I stayed low and focused on keeping my flashlight pointed directly at the helicopter and continued guiding the pilot to our position. As promised, the Vietnamese Marines laid a heavy volume of suppressive fire into the treeline along with the gunships, hoping to give the resupply helo some added protection.

During this second attempt, the helo made it all the way to our pathetic LZ. As it touched down in front of me, the waiting Marines swarmed over the chopper to get the ammo and other supplies. It was a reassuring sight to see this highly trained and motivated unit move into action. We would have our ammo for sure. I moved into the window of the chopper to thank the pilot.

I said, "Smiley 17, great job. We will get you out of here on the same reverse heading. We have another issue, however. Right before you got here we were mortared and took a handful of casualties that need to be medevaced."

After a short pause, he said, "No one said anything about casualties. I'm here to deliver the ammo."

He was right. The need to evacuate casualties had not been part of the original request and I sensed a hesitation on his part to sit on the ground for one more second than necessary. But slowly I got a solid confirmation that picking up the casualties would be ok.

He looked at me and said,"Ok 2 Alpha. Load 'em up. I'm out of here. You owe me a beer."

I turned to the XO and gave him a thumbs up to load the casualties. The prepared Marines loaded them up in minutes. I don't remember how many there were but it was close to the capacity of the chopper. When fully loaded I thanked the pilot again and told him to go back exactly the way he had come. He slowly lifted his precious bird, did a 180 degree turn, and slowly departed along the same direction he had used to come to our assistance a few minutes earlier. I watched his departure for a long time as he stayed close to the ground and slowly went out of sight. I felt relieved to have the ammo and to know our wounded would get medical treatment right away.

After the chopper was gone, the night became incredibly quiet. The day had been so noisy with the air strikes and the fierce firefight. Now with the mortar attack over and the helicopter gone, it was just quiet. I lay on a small rice paddy dike that was reasonably dry. Our two companies were still very exposed but there was no sound from the enemy-occupied treeline. Now that we had our ammunition resupply I felt much better about our chances if the enemy were to assault us during the night. I knew the Vietnamese Marines were ready and totally capable of defending our position. The day had been a frustrating one with the stalemate but we had done well. Our casualties had been medevaced to the rear and we were in position to resume the attack at first light. I believed we had maneuvered our forward elements to where we had the enemy forces right where we wanted them. They were trapped in the treeline with all routes of escape covered by our forces. This was an unusual situation for me. Usually the enemy evaporated after any serious encounter. Again my confidence returned since I had never felt so sure about trapping the enemy before. I was anticipating a clear victory in tomorrow's likely battle.

Looking back on the entire day I decided that we had done ok. Again, The Basic School had prepared me well, this time in the handling of close air support. The Vietnamese had fought hard. We had taken casualties but they didn't seem excessive. Even though we hadn't recovered any enemy dead, we must have hurt their forces badly. They had been pounded by the incredible firepower that came from the close air support aircraft and helicopter gunships. Now we would hold our position against a possible night attack and then have the enemy in our hands in the morning. The only disquieting thought was how the enemy could disengage and get away. A mortar attack was often used as a diversion to allow the enemy forces to organize and move away. Is that what happened with this mortar attack? Was the enemy covering a withdrawal? Could the enemy even get away? We would know in the morning.

CHAPTER 5

ESCAPE

The night continued to be so quiet, too quiet. Compared to the activities of the day before--with the airstrikes, mortar attack and small arms fire-- the night was like another world. I had managed to find a somewhat dry spot on a rice paddy dike and was almost comfortable. I would have preferred to be sleeping in my hammock off the ground but there were no trees and probably the ground was a much safer place to be anyway in case the enemy decided to lob a few more mortars at our position. The Vietnamese Marines were silent as they waited for a possible attack by our trapped enemy or if no attack materialized, an assault into the enemy position at first light.

As dawn approached I grew apprehensive about what was in store for us. I was still convinced that the enemy had been trapped when the battalion moved to cut off the escape routes along the canals. Now we would be able to close on his position from all directions. No question about it, we were at the point of winning a major battle. I knew the firepower of air support was only a phone call away if we needed more of what had been delivered the previous day. I was anxious to find out what would happen when we advanced into the enemy position.

The battalion was up early and on the move. The Vietnamese Marines were cautious yet determined as they moved forward toward the enemy position. I waited for the familiar sound of automatic weapons, expecting the lead elements to come under fire any second. But there was no fire. There was no contact. The enemy was gone. At first I thought it was a joke. What do you mean gone? How could the enemy have gotten out of our trap? These are questions that have never really been answered completely but at least there were theories.

It turned out that the battalion had not totally sealed off all avenues of escape. There was some confusion in the morning as to exactly where the battalion had placed its blocking forces. I had been told the previous night that we had the canals completely covered. Now in the morning I was being told there may have been some holes or gaps. Another explanation was the enemy had slipped away by moving along an intricate network of small waterways which had allowed him to avoid the major canals. I had no idea that such waterways even existed. I wondered if the mortar attack had been a diversion to allow the enemy forces to prepare to move. The confusion of the mortar rounds and the noise of the resupply helicopter could have provided enough distraction to let the enemy slip away in his small watercraft. Regardless of the offered excuses I was crushed. I had been so sure of our success that I had let myself forget the resourcefulness of the enemy and to ignore the realities of trying to catch him. I was sure we had hurt the enemy force but was fearful we would again have little tangible evidence.

As the battalion moved into and through the enemy position in the treeline we found evidence of the previous day's fight. There was plenty of blood and indications that the enemy had been seriously hurt. For awhile we were unable to find any weapons or bodies, but eventually found a makeshift grave with a couple of bodies in it. Nearby we found a couple of weapons. Then there was another find of weapons which were covered with dried blood and three more bodies. We found a total of five enemy dead and ten weapons. That was it for what had been a long intense fight the day before. I told myself the large amount of blood on the ground was proof we had truly hurt the enemy. Also I had seen the enemy "body snatchers" at work when I had been up north. They had a tremendous reputation for not leaving any enemy dead or wounded on the battlefield. I wanted to believe they had dragged off large numbers of their casualties. Why were the bodies so important to me? I guess it was related to the overwhelming sadness when Marines, American or Vietnamese, were killed and wounded. I could see them with their wounds or with their life gone. I wanted to know the enemy had also paid a price and needed to see real proof. It wasn't enough to believe the enemy had suffered casualties just because we had delivered enormous amounts of air power on their position.

By mid morning we had completely searched the area without finding any more enemy dead. The international press flew into our location by chopper to check out the site of the big battle. Military Assistance Command (MACV) representatives came with the press. They interviewed the battalion officers and Major Corah. I don't remember talking to anybody but I am sure I did. After all, it had been a big battle with a tremendous expenditure of air assets. Everyone seemed to know we had just encountered the Viet Cong 261B Main Force Battalion. I had no clue what unit we had fought and really didn't care. I was so disappointed that there was so little to show for it. It had really been a long, hard day and a tough battle. Ten months later I would receive the Silver Star for my part in the fight. But at this moment, as I watched the press move through the area I felt only frustration and painful disappointment. Five bodies, ten weapons and lots of blood were not enough to satisfy my need for a crushing victory.

Shortly after noon we received orders to get ready to move. Intelligence reports said a large enemy unit had been sighted to the west. It was believed to be the same unit that we had engaged the day before. Could it be possible? Would we get another chance at the same unit? The press and higher level MACV folks were gone. We quickly organized the battalion to be ready for another helo assault and moved to a landing zone. Within an hour we were picked up by Army helicopters and flying to another possible rendezvous with the enemy. It was a short helo ride, less than 10 miles. I remember getting in the helo and flying almost at grass-top level as we hurried to our new destination. I sat on the floor of the Huey with my feet hanging out the side, the landing skids of the Huey almost touching the top of the brush as we raced over the terrain of rice paddies and low lying shrubs.

Within minutes we were dropped near another large canal. This time the battalion was together on the same side of the canal. We quickly moved to the bank of the canal and started moving north along the one side. Almost immediately we came to a spot in the canal that had large leafy water plants growing near the bank. The water was very stirred up and murky and the plants were covered with bloody scum. Opposite the water plants and about 25 meters onto the bank were 21 mounds of freshly dug dirt. The mounds were clearly similar in size and placement in parallel rows. The Vietnamese Marines said these were graves. The blood and remains in the water marked the spot where the enemy had washed their dead before burying them. The fact that there were graves indicated that the dead were probably officers and senior enlisted (NCOs) troops. Common soldiers would normally be placed in mass graves rather than individual graves. The conclusion drawn by Major Binh and the other officers was that we had really hurt the enemy unit if there were 21 officers and NCOs killed. This suggested many more soldiers had died in the battle and had been buried somewhere else.

Still I was a doubter. I asked the CO and XO if we could dig up a grave to see exactly what was inside to make sure it contained a body. I can't remember how the conversation went but I do know they said it would be a terrible breach of religion to dig up a body and would not be done. I tried to justify my request by explaining my experiences up north as a platoon leader when we seldom recovered enemy bodies. I didn't push very hard. Some of my frustration at having lost the enemy earlier in the day was reduced when we found the graves. I wanted to believe we had truly hurt the enemy unit during our fight of the day before. I also accepted that respecting the local culture was more important than my need to see bodies. I didn't press the issue.

We didn't stay in the area of the graves for very long. We continued north along both banks of the canal for the rest of the day without any further contact with the enemy. The following day marked the end of the operation and called for our return to a small village. We moved into the hamlet for some badly needed rest.

The battalion continued to operate in the Delta with minor enemy contact. The days were filled with walking patrols as we moved throughout the area looking for any signs of an enemy buildup. Major Corah and I talked on the radio when we were separated for long periods. The pace of operations was steady but the lack of any more serious enemy contact allowed me to think of other things. I started to spend more time thinking about my Rest and Relaxation

(R&R) trip at the end of the month. I had decided to meet Pam in Hawaii. She would arrive one day ahead of me which meant we would have almost six full days together. As January drew to a close I prepared to return to Saigon and then on to Hawaii. I hadn't given much thought to what it would be like to leave Vietnam and go to Hawaii. I had given even less thought to what it would be like to come back to Vietnam after R&R was over. All I knew was that I was leaving at a good time. I felt guilty about leaving the battalion at all but believed I would be gone during a period of no operational activity. Both sides of the war had agreed to a truce during the Vietnamese New Year known as Tet. This truce would cover most of the time I would be away on R&R. I would go to Hawaii and be back before anyone missed me. I did not expect the battalion to be involved in any combat or tactical situations. They would be enjoying the truce in country while I was with Pam in Hawaii. Just like so many times in the past, I was in for more surprises. R&R would turn out to be an incredible emotional challenge, and the Tet Offensive would make a joke out of everyone's plans for a truce, especially mine.

CHAPTER 6

R & R

With Pam Bonsper

I traveled from the Delta back to Saigon in a jeep. A member of the Marine Advisory Unit staff had replaced me in the field. He would act as the assistant advisor with the Second Battalion, Vietnamese Marine Corps until I got back. I was sure he would have a quiet time because of the planned Tet ceasefire. Still I left my unit with mixed emotions. There was the feeling of running out on them for personal reasons. I was going to go off to Hawaii to be with my wife while they would continue in the field fighting. The war had really taken a priority in my life even before I got to Vietnam. As soon as I graduated from the Naval Academy in 1965 I knew that I would eventually be in Vietnam. My arrival was slowed while I spent a year in Costa Rica on a Fulbright Scholarship before attending The Basic School in Quantico, Virginia. But I always knew Vietnam was coming; even my quick marriage to Pam while a student at TBS didn't change anything.

Pam and I had met while I was on the Fulbright in Costa Rica. During summer break (December '65 – March '66) in Costa Rica I decided to travel throughout South America. I used military space-available aircraft to get to Panama; Lima, Peru; and Santiago, Chile. In Chile I linked up with Andy, another student I had met at Georgetown University during our three-week Fulbright preparation course. He had served as an enlisted man in the Navy before completing college in Colorado. At Georgetown we connected because of our military backgrounds. In early January, Andy and I traveled together to Puntarenas, Chile by rail and boat. The boat ride from Puerto Montt to Puntarenas was spectacular as it went through the fiords of the Chilean coast. The entire trip plus a few days in Puntarenas took about 10 days. At that point Andy returned to Santiago by plane and I decided to hitchhike alone to Buenas Aires (BA), Argentina. My trip took me to BA, different cities in Uruguay, and Asuncion, Paraguay. In Asuncion I caught another military flight to Rio de Janeiro. It was there I met Pam, a 19 year-old American who was traveling in Brazil for her own reasons. The short story is that we became good friends and decided to hitchhike together back to Costa Rica. She wanted to see more of South America and I believed having her along would make the hitchhiking easier. The solo hitchhiking I had done to that point: Puntarenas to BA to Montevideo to Punta del Este to Asuncion had convinced me a female partner would make the hitchhiking easier. People were more willing to stop and pick up a couple rather than a solo male. We made the trip together from Rio to San Jose, Costa Rica in 30 days. She returned to the States and I stayed in Costa Rica to finish my

Fulbright. We continued to communicate by Ham radio which allowed our relationship to stay alive even at such a long distance. Pam returned to Costa Rica in June 1966 and rode back to the States with me. We visited her family in Minneapolis, Minnesota and mine in Portville, New York and then parted again to continue with life as it would unfold. I went to Quantico, Virginia in early August to start TBS and within a week knew that I was no longer destined to go through life alone. I called Pam and asked her to marry me over the Labor Day Weekend three weeks away. She said yes and we were married on 3 September 1966.

From the beginning, I told her I would go to Vietnam after my officer training. It wasn't something we talked about and decided together. It was something she had to accept from day one back in Rio. Now I was planning to go on R&R to Hawaii for my personal enjoyment while everyone else stayed in Vietnam. I should have been thrilled for the opportunity to get away from the war and I was. But I also carried some guilt for leaving the Trau Dien who were fighting for the survival of their country.

Pam:

I had been alone since June. Alone in the sense of being without all that mattered, especially the man who had entered my life in such a time and feeling of emptiness, just weeks after my mother died at her own hand. I didn't know anything about grieving and the

72

devastating process of guilt, how it could erode all sense of self and reduce a person's abilities to cope with even the smallest decisions and events. With my marriage and move to Quantico and swift introduction into the life of a military wife, not to mention a decisive and capable husband, I was able to ignore the need to deal with my emptiness and morphed into a proper lieutenant's wife.

When it was time for my healing shield to go to Vietnam, my friend, who I nicknamed Barba, came from Hopkins, Minnesota to live with me until both "our guys" came home. Her husband had earlier gone off to the War and she knew things I didn't. She was just about the best thing that could have happened to me. Together we lived in our little Carmel cottage, newlyweds both, naive young Vietnam War brides, married during a time which tore the country apart.

It was the sixties. Don and I had met each other in Rio de Janeiro and hitch-hiked to Costa Rica. We then drove from Costa Rica to the states. We had tackled the impossible and had overcome incredible obstacles.

We became a married military couple at the chapel in Quantico, Virginia. He went to Basic School and learned how to fight the gooks and I went to teas and coffees and learned which length dress-glove to wear with which length sleeve. He then went to Monterey, California to learn Vietnamese and I stayed home and became the dutiful wife (on the pill, no babies until after the

73

war), wearing bell bottoms and letting my hair grow all one length. On week-ends we drove to San Francisco and watched "the Haight" from Buena Vista Park. High on the hill, we grilled hamburgers on a hibachi and drank cheap wine. The crazy anti-American stoners were down below, spaced out, protesting our war. Lucy in the Sky with Diamonds danced through the trees and tried to sprinkle us with magic but we inhaled wood smoke from our fire. I wore a flower in my hair but did not smell of incense and Patchouli. We sang the lyrics to the songs but did not understand them. The noises down below were louder every time we went to the City. Whirling dervishes, those people were, irresponsible potheads cloaking anger with gaiety.

While our guys were away fighting, my roommate and I stayed away from anything about protests and controversy. We did, however, watch the news for any mention of battle locations and names of key cities. To us, the war was "just"... and just was. Nothing we could do about it and we certainly weren't trying to follow the politics. Our theory was the domino theory; our men were killing the evil Communists who were taking over the world. We knew where our men stood on the subject and we stood behind them. We supported them by believing what they believed. We supported them by looking for jobs, writing letters, making reel-to-reel voice tapes, sending care packages and preparing for R&R. We were the patriotic, the righteous and the dutiful.

74

As we pulled into Saigon from the Delta the city looked the same to me as it had when I had first joined the MAU in November. It was busy with all kinds of vehicular traffic and people hurrying everywhere. I wondered just how much these people appreciated what was going on out in the field. The city appeared to be full of energy as everyone prepared to celebrate the Lunar New Year. I had the rest of that day and all the next day to get ready for my R&R flight to Hawaii. That meant I also had two glorious nights to sleep in my room at the Splendid BOQ. It had been almost two months since I had last slept in my bed. Being in the BOQ also meant I could enjoy the company of other military officers in the bar. It was like living a normal life.

I had been on the grapefruit diet too long. If I looked at another hard-boiled egg, I was going to turn green. But Barba reminded me that R&R was only two days away and according to the plan, I could optimally lose 4 more pounds. It wasn't so hard during the day when I was in class (taking courses at the local community college) but in the evening I lost all willpower. I stopped at the store on the way to my night shift as a PBS operator and bought a package of Oreos, a bag of chips and a diet rite cola.

It didn't take long to put my few civilian clothes in a bag and to get cleaned up. I had managed to buy a present for Pam while I was in Okinawa during the time I had been transferred from my assignment with the US Marines in I Corps en route to the MAU which would serve as a belated Christmas present. The two days and nights in Saigon were like a halfway house for me. Saigon was clearly different from the field (combat areas) and Hawaii (no war) was going to be different from Saigon (war). The decision to meet Pam in Hawaii had been a hard one. Many of the Marine officers in Vietnam chose to take their R&R in other parts of Asia or Australia. They went alone or with other Marines rather than meet their wives or girl friends in Hawaii or anywhere else. The reasons varied but often it was because they didn't want to be with their wives or girl friends for a few days and then have to leave them again. It seemed better to go off to Thailand, Australia, Taipei, or Hong Kong and just forget the war and all other responsibilities. When I left California and went to Vietnam I had entertained the thought of not taking my R&R in Hawaii primarily because of the cost. I knew Pam and I could use the money in so many other important ways once I got home. The unexpected promotion to Captain, however, had increased my salary and really provided some "new" money for R&R. Plus within a few days of my arrival in Vietnam I knew that if I was still alive, I would have to take advantage of the R&R opportunity to see Pam. The pain of the separation had been so unforeseen that I had started questioning the plan to skip R&R. As the days and months passed I slowly realized there was no way I would not see my wife in Hawaii. Now the time had come. My bag was packed and I was waiting to board the plane at Than San Nhut airport that would carry me to Honolulu.

Packing was a major event. Everything had to be what he would like. Miniskirts were now in. Don had never seen me in one, but I packed one, hoping he would approve. I carefully folded and unfolded, tucking clothing around a double batch of chocolate chip cookies which I had packed in a large tin. At least I had my dear friend with me on packing night. She had already been to Hawaii to meet her husband so she was a veteran. While we stayed up late and made sure everything was just right, she told me what to wear, what to do, and what to see while on the romantic island of Oahu. What she didn't tell me was what she shouldn't tell me, and I didn't want to know that anyway. This was to be the trip I had looked forward to for almost eight months. It was to be a fun adventure: exotic, romantic, and all that my friend pretended to me that night.

I don't remember much about the plane ride except the stewardesses. They were real women who smiled and laughed and asked us about our plans for R&R. The plane was full of supercharged men heading to Hawaii for a few days with their wives, girlfriends, or parents. We were all nervous about what lay ahead since there would be so little time. We would have six nights together. Somehow the nights seemed more important than the days. In my case, I remembered another time when I had been separated from Pam. That was before we were married. We had separated after our hitchhiking adventure from Rio de Janeiro, Brazil to San Jose, Costa Rica so she could return to her home in Minnesota and I could return to my studies at the University of San Jose in Costa Rica. She was coming back to Costa Rica so she could travel with me, in my car, back to the States. This was her idea. At first I was unsure if this would work since I had already planned a route back to my home with a series of stops along the way. Something told me to tell her it was a great idea and to come to Costa Rica and we would make the trip back to the States together. Then that day I had waited for her at the airport in San Jose, Costa Rica, standing on the observation roof so I would have a good view of her when she debarked from the airplane. I was so concerned about how she would look. Would I recognize her? Would she stand out? Would she give me the energy she had given before? Yes! Pam emerged looking great and we had spent beautiful days in San Jose preparing for our return to the States.

Now as I prepared to land in Hawaii, the tables were turned. Pam would be there waiting for me. We had planned the time so she would arrive in Hawaii one day ahead of me. This would give her time to get settled in the hotel without having to waste the time we would have together. The departure plans were the same. I would leave Hawaii first when R&R ended, again giving us as much time together as possible. The plane bounced onto the runway causing a loud cheer from all of us aboard. Our dream of leaving Vietnam for a few precious days with our loved ones was coming true.

Everything was in order. I had only two hangnails that had been chewed so badly I couldn't cover them up. The ride to San Francisco was so uneventful I can't even remember if my roommate drove me or if I took a plane out of Monterey; it was uneventful or maybe I was just too nervous. I do remember, on the other hand, many details about the plane ride from San Francisco to Hawaii. For one thing, I sat next to myself except she was blond and taller and just a bit more made up than I was. Her husband was in the Army instead of the Marine Corps. We talked about where our guys were fighting and what we would do in Hawaii. But they were just words. We both wanted to say, I don't give a care about you or your husband or the girl behind me's husband.

There was just one person that mattered to each of us, each of the nervous young women, some even younger than I. I was twenty and wearing "Shalimar." That seemed important as Don had given it to me for Christmas. As I crossed the Pacific Ocean in that big steel bird, I only thought about one person. I struggled to bring his presence back to me. I leaned my head against the headrest, closed my eyes and thought about his deep blue eyes, the rough stubble on his face in the morning, his broad shoulders that had so often become pillows as we traveled across the thousands of miles. I then thought of the picture he sent from Vietnam. He was bare-chested, his ribs stuck out, he looked emaciated and bewildered. It had been taken after many days in the jungle and he looked like a stranger. But I forced the reasons for these changes out of my head. I pushed them away and did not want to think of other possible changes. Everything would be just like before.

Twenty minutes before landing was panic time. One hundred young women, mixed in with some other kinds of people we couldn't see, were all putting on just a little bit more eye shadow, then going through their make-up cases realizing they forgot to bring something. Why we were so concerned, I don't know. For the most part we were arriving before our men and we wouldn't see them until the following day. The stewardesses knew about these flights, knew about them because their fiancés or their boyfriends or their brothers were over there too. They were firm about the seatbelts and with twenty minutes until landing, we were all safely in our places, all with silent prayers on our lips and visions of that one person in our minds.

We landed. We were on the ground and the hot balmy air brought us to another land. Young Hawaiian girls with hula skirts placed flowers around our necks just as if we had come to Hawaii for a vacation. Still there were no men. We soon lost our adhesion as suddenly we were pulled apart by different colored taxis and different destinations. It was night. I had to get myself (who should be and soon would be "us") to the hotel. And get it ready.

Getting a room ready that is already painfully ready takes a long time. I placed the cookie tin on the little kitchenette counter. I unpacked my clothes, one by one, and looked at the bikini pajamas and wondered if he would like them. I touched up my nails, knowing that he didn't like nail polish, but it just somehow seemed right that for R&R and not having seen each other for so long, I should wear polish. I washed my hair that night which was dumb, because I didn't have a hair dryer and even if I could have slept, which I couldn't, I wouldn't have because my hair was so wet. But somehow I got through that awful, more lonely than ever night. The next morning I got ready for three hours and left for the airport where I would be reunited with Don.

Whoever was in charge of R&R reunions knew what they were doing. Or maybe it hadn't been done in the beginning months of the war, but now they were prepared. A tall man in a dark suit, a Bible in one hand, was greeting us women as we entered the airport. We all looked around to see who he was there for.

The plane came to a stop and we all tried to act so casual as we picked up our carry-on items. The open door of the airplane let in the balmy air of Hawaii. It was mid afternoon. The day was clear and

81

sunny. As we walked into the terminal we were greeted by a shout from the waiting wives and girlfriends. It was incredible. Only hours earlier we had been in various locations throughout a country at war. Now we were in a U.S. paradise. Again I felt the pangs of guilt, as though I had been allowed to leave a football game which was being played in the freezing rain and mud, to take a hot shower, put on a warm, dry, clean uniform before returning to play the second half. There in the crowd of women was Pam. She looked beautiful to me. Again I had been so worried about how she would look but had never given any thought to how I would look to her. It's funny now to remember how selfish I had been. She had to live up to my expectations in so many ways. She would have to accept me however I was. I can't remember if I went through customs but whatever I had to do didn't take very long. Soon we were embracing and kissing and crying. We were together. But then the practical, organized part of my personality took over. We had to get going to the hotel. Time was wasting. We got my checked luggage and headed outside to get a taxi. Pam gave directions to the hotel and off we went. R&R had officially begun.

The chaplain was talking to all of us. At first I couldn't figure out why. But then he used words like "expectations" and "circumstances changing" and "sudden emergencies." Oh my God, I thought, is he really saying sometimes the plane lands and a husband that was supposed to be on it, isn't? I remember feeling a sense of betrayal at this and suddenly felt like crying. Within a short time, two women were singled out and the chaplain took them aside. I knew from that moment on that the island of Oahu in 1968 was for some an empty desolate rock of cold volcanic ash.

The rest of us felt sorry for the young women while simultaneously experiencing a selfish sense of personal relief. While straining our ears for some sign of the approaching plane we collectively leaned in the direction of the arriving aircraft in an attempt to rid ourselves of any unpleasantness. We let out a deafening scream when the plane landed and all of us pressed our faces to the window glass. As soon as the men came through the door, the chaplain had told us, we could meet them. We were not allowed to go through the window or knock down the velveteen ropes that led out to the arrival area. We did obey the window rule, but as soon as the first man walked into the building, the ropes could not hold us. We ran like a pack of starving wolves. When I saw Don he looked more handsome than I had even remembered, and when he dropped his bag to engulf me in his arms I began shaking and couldn't seem to stop.

The next few days were a blur. We rented a car and drove everywhere. We made a trip around the entire island, stopping whenever and wherever we wanted. There was plenty of time at the beach enjoying the beautiful white sand and warm water. We visited many of the tourist attractions during the day and hit the night spots after dark. It was great to be together again but we really weren't totally together and certainly not alone. Something was with us that is hard to describe. Maybe it was like a dark cloud hanging over us no matter where we went or what we did. In any moment of pleasure or happiness there was a voice reminding me that Hawaii was not my current home. There was the full knowledge that this was only a temporary respite from the war; that time was ticking away until I would have to climb aboard a plane and return to Vietnam. Somehow the fact that R&R in Hawaii would be such a short time only added to the pressure and tension of our reunion. Still, I told myself we were together and no matter how short the time we had, we would make the most of it.

I wished he could relax. Sure, we had only six days, but did we have to do and see everything in such an organized way? I had the feeling this was a maneuver he was executing, like reaching the hill before nightfall. On the other hand, as always, I was grateful for his take charge attitude and just happy to have him with me. He talked very little about the war and I asked very little. We were just a couple of young tourists going to the Polynesian shows and driving by the pineapple farms.

I think it was our second or third night that we went to Duke

Kahanamoku's to have dinner and see the Don Ho show. Don Ho was a singer who strongly supported the U.S. servicemen who were fighting in Vietnam. His show was full of patriotic music and open praise for Vietnam veterans who were in the audience. Actually, the vast majority of the people at the club were husbands and wives who were on R&R. Pam and I arrived at the club prepared to have a good time. The first couple of days of R&R had gone well even though there was a feeling of unexplained and undiscussed tension. We ordered our meals and sat back to enjoy the jokes, music, and atmosphere of the Don Ho Show.

I was so anxious to go to Duke Kahanamoku's. This was THE place to go if you went nowhere else. I had heard my roommate talk about it and just knew this would be the night I should wear my new pink mini-dress. I was so excited to be going somewhere so expensive and so romantic. We had been living on pennies. The Marine Corps didn't have housing for families of men who deployed, so almost all of Don's income went to my rent and utilities. We did get the whopping one dollar a day separation pay, but that didn't go far. I had found a horrible part-time job working nights as a switch-board operator, so we had enough, and Don was salting anything extra away for a new car, but still, we were being very thrifty and had not even gone on a honeymoon in anticipation of added expenses when Don was overseas. As he told me once, "If the Marine Corps wanted

us to have wives, they would have issued them." It was up to us to
make do with what he got.

*Now, we were splurging "to the max" and probably spending
more in one night than we had in a whole month.*

As was probably inevitable, the smallest thing resulted in a fight. I
had always been a big eater, consuming two lunches every day in the
high school cafeteria. The appetite stayed with me through the Naval
Academy and into our marriage. Whenever Pam and I went out to
eat I would usually finish whatever she didn't eat. Sometimes I think
she pretended to be full just so there was something extra for me.
This night Pam had not been able to finish her salad, but rather than
pass the salad to me, she had allowed the waitress to take the remains
of her salad away. I exploded. Why? I have no idea. All of a sudden
it seemed important that she had not given me the opportunity to
finish the salad. It wasn't that I was going hungry. Rather it was a
combination of my always trying to be cost/effective and of our
working together on things. I told her I thought she was wrong or
careless or something to let the salad get away. She reacted as she
should have. She was incredulous that I could have bothered about
such a small thing when there were so many more important things
to worry about. Still we argued. That ruined the rest of the night at
the club. Dinner arrived and was consumed. The show came and
went and finally we were back at the hotel. Exercising great maturity,

I took a pitcher of homemade Mai Tais down to the pool where I decided I would drown my hurt. After a couple of hours of acting like a baby, I returned to the motel room where Pam and I were able to resolve the ridiculous problem. At least the emotional dam had broken. Now we could get on with the remaining days of R&R.

Don looked so "squared away" and irresistibly handsome as he sat across the table from me. In the background, the Duke was singing "Tiny Bubbles," one of his most famous songs. Some of the other couples were singing along and swaying to the music. Some had started to dance. It was a beautiful restaurant with colored lights and exotic tropical flowers just everywhere. Fancy food was being served on fancy plates. But I was so excited I could hardly eat. I wanted the evening to last forever and not think about why we seemed to be acting like strangers at times. After all, this was the most romantic place to be and I would be able to tell the wives back home (who were still waiting for their R&R's) all about it. Suddenly I looked up from my salad plate which the waitress was removing and realized I had done something terribly wrong. Don was mad. The trembling began again but this time it was happening inside. On the outside I got through the evening and knowing how expensive it was, even faked having a good time. We returned to our little hotel cabana in almost utter silence. I felt as if I had been stabbed by a knife. I cried for hours while Don sat by the pool.

As I lay alone on the bed, I wondered what had happened to our wonderful experience in Waikiki. I did not know then that it was not about a stupid salad but instead about a surreal concept. Somehow the US military had decided it would be beneficial to the war effort to pluck a Marine grunt out of the jungles or rice paddies or wherever the heck he was and fly him to the island of Oahu and put him out under a full moon in Waikiki with his sweetie. He wouldn't have changed nor would she. They would kiss and make love then he would be plucked out of their Shangri-la and plopped back down in the muck. Back to being a killer, back to eating c-rats, digging holes, blowing up the enemy, ducking mortar rounds, picking up body parts and stuffing them in bags.

I should have realized then that my tears were really much deeper than getting my feelings hurt. They were tears that had been building up for months: tears of abandonment, resentment, fear, and loneliness. They were tears for my family--for my father and brothers I felt I had abandoned--for the friends back home who had been told their husbands had been killed, for the POWs on TV who were being dragged through the streets as war trophies, for the women who had been at the airport, the ones who had been pulled aside by the chaplain, and for the men who were supposed to be on that plane.

I didn't realize those things then. I just cried alone as our precious moments, our long-awaited precious moments, just silently and slowly and steadily ticked away.

The next couple of days were filled with sightseeing and fun and passed quickly. The day before I was to return to Vietnam, we heard the news about the Tet Offensive. The newspapers and television were full of stories about how the North Vietnamese Army (NVA) and Viet Cong (VC) had been able to infiltrate large numbers of troops into Saigon itself. The media made it sound like Saigon would fall any minute. I was stunned. First, I didn't believe the news was accurate. Second, I doubted that the enemy could afford to come out in the open in such numbers. Pam became worried about my having to return. It was one thing to talk about going back to a place where there was a truce being observed. Going to a city that was under a major attack was a completely different story. The tension we had felt earlier now returned with a renewed intensity. At first Pam thought I would have to stay in Hawaii until things calmed down in Vietnam and Saigon. Not so. R&R would end on schedule and there were no postponements of my flight.

After that horrible night things were better. It was hard to completely forget the war no matter how hard we tried and it was hard to ignore the changes in both of us. We were walking back to the hotel from the Aquarium one afternoon and suddenly there was a backfire from a passing car. Don dropped to the ground and pulled me with him. People walking by looked at us like we were nuts. We joked about it and he seemed embarrassed. It never happened again during R&R and he never had nightmares--the middle of the night wake-ups that I had seen in war movies--during our few nights together. He adjusted to normal big-city noises and slept soundly. This was important to me. I didn't want him to be weird. I had thought about all kinds of things when I was back in Carmel. What if he was captured and became a POW? What if he was tortured? What would it do to him? I was scared because I didn't know how the things he had seen and done would affect him.

Now I was scared because there seemed to be a build up in the news and Don was listening intently. The days were down to two. He was supposed to be returning to a peaceful interlude of no fighting, but he still had many more months of combat. He hadn't told me of his numerous and miraculous close-calls, but I sensed he had been through Hell. And there was a lot more to come. In the still quiet of bed that night I told him that it didn't matter if he lost his arms and legs and came back home to me in a wheelchair. I just didn't want him to lose his mind because then he wouldn't be Don anymore. And I needed him to be him. I guess I must have realized that his adjustment to loud noises was deliberate and his nightmares were screamed in a lonely silence. I knew mine were.

The last day and night were the hardest. Actually we had known from the very beginning that I would have to go back. The knowledge that we had six days, then five, then four, and so on had weighed heavily on our minds. It had been impossible to truly enjoy the time together when we knew it would end in just a few more days. But the last day and night were the worst, and the news of the Tet Offensive only added to the tension and fear we both felt.

He assured me it wasn't that bad. He talked about things like the car and whether I had enough money and when to have the oil changed. He said he had had a couple of close calls but God would protect him and we just had to get through a few more months and it would be over. I listened to him, wanting to believe every word, while in the background the TV kept talking about the enormous attacks throughout the country during Tet.

Pam and I got up that last morning and started the process which eventually led us to the airport and my flight. We talked of my going back for only a little over four more months and then my coming home to California. We didn't know about our next assignment within the Marine Corps but knew it would be better than the war and this separation. Pam was very strong and professional as we wasted the final minutes in the airport. I felt so sick to my stomach that I wondered if I would have been better off to skip R&R altogether. I didn't know it then, but there would be three more long separations in my future. This would be my one and only R&R. We hugged, kissed, cried, and finally said goodbye. She would catch her flight within a couple of hours after I had departed. I climbed aboard the airplane and was soon on my way back to Vietnam and the Crazy Water Buffalo Battalion. I looked at my Zodiac Seawolf and reminded the durable watch that we still had some time to go before we would return home.

Don had not worn his uniform the entire time in Hawaii. When he put it on to go to the airport, I had a feeling I shouldn't touch him. He belonged to someone else now and all of his gestures were somehow related to the uniform, how he tucked his cover (flat hat) under his belt, how he centered his belt buckle, how he held the bags and returned salutes to fellow servicemen. I became an observer to this squared away professional. I suddenly felt frightfully inadequate to be a Marine Officer's wife. All of the frivolous concerns that had absorbed my attention just days ago seemed to have been buried under thousands of pounds of debris. The dress style, hairdo, and how much I weighed were far off in some unreachable direction. Domino theory, Viet Cong informers, the DMZ and the morality of our involvement were pushing their way into my consciousness. I obediently went through the motions of a good send-off and "Sure I'll be alright," as we held each other in a final embrace. But I knew I would never be the same again and if he ever came back he better have more than his mind.

He better have his arms and legs.

The flight back was totally different from the flight from Vietnam to Hawaii. The stewardesses didn't seem as friendly or as willing to ask us about the areas we were going back to in Vietnam. On the flight over they asked about who we were meeting in Hawaii and how long we had been apart. Now they were all business. The food was average and there was a sadness permeating the entire airplane. None of the returning servicemen was in the mood to make jokes or act happy. The pure fact of the situation was we were going back to war and we were going farther away from the ones we loved. I settled into my seat and tried to prepare myself mentally for what was waiting in Saigon and the rest of Vietnam. I had left my battalion in the Delta. I would have to land first in Saigon and then rejoin the battalion, wherever it was. I still believed the stories about the enemy attack had been exaggerated. My previous experiences of reading newspaper accounts about operations I had been on made me think that this would be another example of overboard sensational reporting. As the plane made its final approach into Saigon I steeled myself for what lay ahead. And like so many times before, I was in for more surprises.

And then he was gone. It was that fast. There was no one to carry my suitcase and no one to walk beside, just a huge cold airport full of

93

people who wore no faces. I had a feeling of weak fragility and abject fear, an emptiness so deep I could hardly breathe. I wanted to grab somebody...anybody! Where was the chaplain? Where was a friend? Where was an answer to why he was gone? For several minutes I sat alone in the airport, unable to adjust to not having him with me. I remember just sitting there holding my face in my hands, staring at the cold tile floor and feeling nauseated. I looked out at the empty place in the sky where I'd had a last glimpse of his plane and just waited. Little by little the tears surfaced. I silently asked that he please, please come back home to me. I looked up and down the immense airport. Groups of anxious wives were running for the arrival gate; stick-straight men in uniform, stoic frozen faces on toy soldiers, were heading for the departure gates.

I blew my nose and stuffed the tissue in my purse. I looked again up and down the airport. It was filled with people, people coming and going to Oahu for rest and relaxation. I had no idea what time it was and Don and his time-perfect watch were not there. I stood up and looked for a sign with directions to United Airlines and tried to think of just exactly what... what it was I was supposed to do next.

CHAPTER 7

SURPRISE REUNION

R&R was over. It had come and gone too fast. The 6 days had evaporated like steam from a wet log on a hot day. Now I was back in Vietnam. I felt so lousy on the plane ride back to Vietnam that I wasn't sure if meeting Pam had been a good idea. The departure in the airport had been painful and strained. Our distress at having to separate again was only magnified by the volume of news about the Tet Offensive that had surprised the country on 31 January. The Tet Offensive included a series of surprise attacks by the Vietcong and North Vietnamese forces on scores of cities, towns, and hamlets throughout South Vietnam. It was considered to be a turning point in the Vietnam War.

North Vietnamese leaders believed they could not sustain the heavy losses inflicted by the Americans indefinitely and had to win the war with an all-out military effort. In addition, Ho Chi Minh was nearing death, and they needed a victory before that time came. The combined forces of the Vietcong and the North Vietnamese Regular Army, about 85,000 strong, launched a major offensive throughout South Vietnam.

The attacks began on 31 January 1968, the first day of the Lunar New Year, Vietnam's most important holiday and one day before I was scheduled to return to Vietnam. It took weeks for U.S. and South Vietnamese troops to retake all of the captured cities, including the former imperial capital of Hue. Even though the offensive was a military failure for the North Vietnamese Communists and Vietcong (VC), it was a political and psychological victory for them because it dramatically contradicted optimistic claims by the U.S. government that the war was all but over. But that was all behind me. I was on the ground at Tan Son Nhut airport and would soon be back with the Second Battalion, Vietnamese Marine Corps (VNMC), or so I thought.

As I got out of the plane and headed for the terminal to get my bag, I could hear the sounds of combat in the distance. There were both small arms fire and the sounds of either artillery or mortars. The airport was full of military police and regular military personnel. All carried weapons and all looked worried. My reluctance to believe that all of this was happening made me look for evidence that would say these people were overreacting. After all, I had seen "real" combat in the field. This was just the typical reaction of people who were used to the security of the rear and who now had to face the realities of the war, wasn't it?

I got my checked bag and looked for a way to get from the airport into Saigon. I was told that it was too dangerous to go to the city at that time. I would have to wait until the road was declared safe for civilian and commercial vehicles. Military vehicles were allowed however, to drive to the city. No one had met me at the airport from the Marine Advisory Unit but I hadn't expected anyone. I had not communicated with the unit while I was in Hawaii and had not been able to tell anyone exactly the time of my arrival. I walked around the outside of the airport looking for a jeep or other vehicle that might be going to the city. I found a jeep which had a couple of military personnel with M-16s getting ready to drive into Saigon. They appeared to have room for me and my bag. I walked up to the jeep and hoped for the best.

"Are you heading into Saigon and do you have room for one more?" I asked.

"Yes, we are," they replied. "Where are you headed?"

"I need to get to the Splendid BOQ."

"You're in luck. We pass the Splendid on our way to our home base. Jump in and hang on."

I had no weapon but didn't really feel I would need one. The guys in the jeep had M16s which would certainly suffice as we moved along the road to the city. If we ran into trouble I would just do my best to find cover while they defended us and the jeep. If one of them became a casualty I would use his weapon. I was still in denial about the serious nature of the situation.

We drove from the airport to Saigon with no problem. This was the third day of the offensive so I guess I was seeing just the tail end of the attack on the airport and the city. After being dropped off at the BOQ, I coordinated with the front desk to let them know I was back from Hawaii and would be using my room for at least a day or two. I organized my gear for the field, notified the MAU that I was back and prepared to rejoin my unit whenever necessary. I did manage to get another night of sleep in my bed. It was good to have this one night in a bed to act like another halfway house or transition back to the real world of operational combat.

The next morning I went first to the MAU headquarters where I was told I would not be rejoining Second Battalion right away but would instead be working with a separate company from another battalion because of the operational situation. This would be a temporary assignment until Saigon was cleaned up and back to normal. The new company was located on the northeast side of the city near a small bridge. As fate would have it, the company was commanded by Lieutenant Day.

Normally the name of the commanding officer of the company would not make any difference to me. There were six VNMC battalions, each with a full complement of officers. During my time in Vietnam I had seen very little of the other battalions so I didn't know many of their officers. But Lt. Day was an exception. I had known him since The Basic School in Quantico. When I realized I would be working with him after my return from R&R I had to think back to our time together at TBS.

TBS had been a very serious time for me. I left the Naval

Academy in 1965 as a young know-it-all who truly enjoyed having a good time. Had I gone to TBS at that time I am sure I would have been less serious. But I went from the academy to Latin America for a year on the Fulbright Scholarship. That year had a tremendous effect on me. First, I was able to get rid of four years of academy limited freedom with no trouble. Second, the year in Latin America helped me start to grow up. And finally, it was during that year that I met Pam and decided that I had found the woman I wanted to marry. So I arrived at TBS with my wild oats already sown. I was there to learn about the Marine Corps and to prepare for going to Vietnam.

My sad personal problem was that I thought everyone should be as serious as I was. If someone was unable to keep up on the physical training runs, I felt it was my duty to encourage him to try harder. If he didn't make what I thought was an honest effort then I openly accused him of being a quitter or slacker. We had nine Vietnamese Marine officers in my basic school class. As a group they did not seem to be as motivated as I thought they should be. I felt that we were preparing to go and fight in their country yet they weren't really serious about the training at TBS. Maybe they already knew enough about war. Maybe TBS was a welcome relief for them from the horrors of their own country. I didn't think about any of that then; I only criticized them for not trying hard enough. One of those young Vietnamese officers was Lieutenant Day.

We had been organized by platoon at TBS according to our last name. Bonsper and Day were both in First Platoon of Company C. Since we were in the same platoon, we were together for all field and platoon physical training. I was hard on Lt. Day. I called him a quitter and I suppose many other things. When I think back on it now, I wonder who I thought I was that I could be so demanding and critical of him and his other officers. He was tall, strong and spoke excellent English. I felt he was totally capable of doing better. Right or wrong I pushed Day to try harder. He responded by telling me if I ever got to Vietnam he "would kill me." That didn't seem like a real threat at the time since I was destined to be a platoon leader with the U.S. Marines. But now as the jeep bumped down the gritty track of a dirt road to join Lt. Day and his company, ironically to serve as his advisor, I wondered how he would feel about seeing me show up in his unit.

As I prayed would happen, he let me drive into his position without gunning me down. We talked about Basic School and what had happened. I now understood much better what he had left to come to the United States to attend TBS and why he might have been less serious than I thought was appropriate. I had changed a great deal since leaving Quantico and so had he. Now he was a company commander and I was his temporary advisor. I did my best to apologize for my arrogance and criticism of his performance at TBS. He graciously accepted my apology.

I stayed with his company for almost two weeks. He impressed me with his tactical knowledge and attention to detail. We operated within a small sector on the northeast side of Saigon with minor enemy contact. We captured a couple of prisoners and accounted for a few enemy dead but never encountered any major enemy forces. The Tet Offensive in and around Saigon had been short lived. The enemy had attacked the presidential palace, the airport, the ARVN headquarters, and fought their way onto the U.S. Embassy grounds. The U.S. and ARVN forces, which were caught off guard, quickly responded and within a week had recouped most of the lost territory. Hue was a different story, however, as the Vietcong held their ground. I talked with other members of the MAU who described the initial enemy attacks which had resulted in very heavy casualties on the part of the Viet Cong and North Vietnamese Army. They told me of human wave-like assaults across bridges and roads leading into Saigon. The enemy soldiers were easily defeated and unable to gain any real foothold in the city. Again I wondered why the enemy had been so foolish to attack in such large numbers when they were so effective in small unit operations. Of course the political impact of the Tet Offensive was something I never even considered in 1968. I just saw the massive attack as a giant tactical mistake by the NVA and VC. But in other parts of the country, like Hue City, the battle raged on and on. The strategic value of Tet and its political repercussions made a huge difference later in the war. When General Westmorland asked for

200,000 more troops to finish the war the country slowly changed from mostly supporting the war effort to making sure it was ended.

After a couple of weeks with Lt. Day, I returned to the Second Battalion and within a few days we were again back in the Mekong Delta having made the trip in trucks and other vehicles. Like before, we would be operating in the territory controlled by the Army of Vietnam (ARVN) with helicopter support from the U.S. Army. I had been back from R&R for almost three weeks and was firmly back in an operational mode. The civilian experience of being in Hawaii with Pam for six wonderful days was a faded memory that was disappearing quickly.

CHAPTER 8

CARELESS

We returned to the same pattern of operating for 3-5 days and then moving into small villages for a day or two of rest. This was the same way we had operated before I went on R&R and the battalion was recalled to Saigon for the Tet Offensive. After moving into a small village or hamlet, the battalion commander would talk to the village chief and the battalion would just establish a position in and around the village. We provided some protection to the village and also bought food and other items from the people. In my experience the relationship between the members of the battalion and the local villages was always positive. The Marines paid for what they took and seemed to be respected by the villagers.

We always seemed to find something on every operation. We didn't have any major contact that compared to our fight in early January but usually had at least one firefight which resulted in enemy prisoners or captured weapons. The battalion usually did a quick interrogation of the prisoners and then turned them over to the ARVN command. They were treated humanely while under battalion control, receiving food, water, and cigarettes. Time passed quickly for me since we were always on the move. It was a treat to arrive in a small village and be able to find some "Bier Larue" or "Ba Muoi Ba"

(Beer 33). The heat and humidity of Vietnam made a cold beer seem like a forbidden treasure. All beer came in bottles. Of course there wasn't any refrigeration in the small villages so the beer had to be cooled with chunks of ice. The ice was in large blocks which were packed in sawdust and burlap sacks. We would buy a bottle of beer, get a glass, and then chip off a chunk of ice with our knives. A little water would clean off the dust and dirt from the outside of the ice but the creatures and debris that had been frozen inside were still there. Somehow the presence of this extra "bonus" element of the ice didn't seem important enough to avoid using the ice. But it usually meant that you didn't drink your glass of beer down to the last drop. There was always something that had settled to the bottom that was best thrown away. That habit still stays with me today when I drink a glass of water. I just can't drink the entire glass, no matter how thirsty. I will drink most of the glass, throw out the little that remains and refill the glass if I am still thirsty. I am always suspicious there is something in the bottom.

During part of our time in the Delta (IV Corps) there were two infantry battalions, the artillery unit, and a task force headquarters all operating close to each other. This meant we had 6-8 advisors who were able to get together when we were not actually on an operation. I always looked forward to any chance to talk with other members of the MAU. This time we were also within two hours of driving to an Army Special Forces compound which had U.S. food, beer, hot water, and a small post exchange (PX) which was like a mini department store. Each PX around the world is different but each has items of value to the local clients. We would never find cold-weather clothing in Vietnam. But we would find junk food, cigarettes, lighters, appropriate kinds of clothing, and so on. The temptation to visit the compound with its obvious benefits was much stronger than our concerns about the obvious dangers of driving across the Delta for two hours in a jeep.

We worked out a plan where we would send two jeeps with two advisors in each vehicle with a Vietnamese Marine driver. Our routine would have the two-jeep convoy leave first thing in the morning and return in late afternoon. Since there were eight of us all together, we each had a chance to visit the compound every two days. Usually we would have two days between operations so it worked out so everyone had an opportunity to make the trip every time we stood down after an operation. If we only had one day between operations we knew who was next to visit the compound.

I do not honestly remember how many trips we had made since arriving in the Delta. Since our "local village" location was always different, the visit to the compound would use different roads. The actual distance and driving time would vary but it usually meant a trip of about two hours each way.

All I remember is I didn't get to go on the next trip. Four other advisors executed our plan and made the trip to the compound and back with no problems. They told us they saw plenty of local villagers and farmers along the road but no one appeared to pay any attention to them. They drove fast and didn't stop for anything. While at the compound they got hot showers, drank plenty of cold beer and chowed down on American food. All four of them reported the trip was worth the two hours of travel each way in the jeep. The following day, the artillery advisor, Major Jim Bennett, medical advisor, Lieutenant Commander Tom "Doc" Anderson, regimental advisor, Lieutenant Colonel Roger McKinley, and I made the next trip. We left around 0900 and had no problem finding the compound following a new road from our village. The trip was uneventful just like the day before. Major Bennett and I shared one jeep and "Doc" Anderson and LtCol McKinley shared the other. There were plenty of people walking along the road or working in the rice paddies. We just sailed by like we didn't have a care in the world. We all carried our pistols while the drivers had their M-16 rifles. The longer we drove the less attention we paid to the world around us. We were decompressing without even knowing what was happening. We were on a "road trip" to a safe, enjoyable paradise in the middle of a war. The time at the compound was fantastic. I took the longest hot shower of my life and ate and drank myself to excess. I can't remember everything we did but it was a pleasant break from the normal operational routine. We actually enjoyed ourselves too much both by drinking more than was smart and by staying later than we should have. I do remember something about dancing and singing on a long bar while the Army Special Forces patrons laughed and cheered me on. I reverted to a college fraternity member, acting like an idiot rather than the combat-tested veteran of 24 that I really was. The release from the daily stress and tension was just too strong which made it so hard to leave and accept that we had to go back to our units. The delay almost ruined everything.

When we finally did start the trip back to our unit it was late in the afternoon, too late. We would have to hurry in order to be back before it started to get dark. Not to worry. We loaded up the jeeps with some junk food and other items we were able to buy in the PX and headed west. This time the roads were almost empty so there wasn't anything to slow us down. As we sailed across the Delta, looking at the flat terrain of the rice paddies, I had the feeling of almost having fun. It was as though the war wasn't really out there. We were just a bunch of regular guys going back to the office after a long, wet lunch. The people smiled, waved, or just ignored us as we flew by. Then it all ended.

In just a few seconds I was rocked back to reality. There was a large explosion from the left and behind us. Jim and I were in the lead jeep with the second jeep about 10 meters behind. I looked back at the other jeep and it was still there. We pulled over to the side of the road and skidded to a stop. Jim grabbed the driver's M-16 and jumped out of the jeep. We thought we saw some people running away from us out in the rice paddy. They were at least a couple of hundred meters away and were heading into a treeline.

Jim said, "Those SOBs. They can't do this to us. I am going to get them. They will pay."

He started to move toward the rice paddy but stopped when common sense kicked in. In spite of our reduced ability to reason and be smart, I knew we could not go chasing anybody across a rice paddy. So did Jim. Almost immediately the occupants of the second jeep came up to us and asked what had happened. Their arrival was key to our later decisions. They had taken more of the brunt of the explosion than we had. The front windshield of their jeep had been destroyed and "Doc" Anderson had blood coming from his left ear. No one else had been injured but the concussion of the blast had taken its toll.

We stood in the road for a few minutes shaking off the effects of the noisy blast and the afternoon booze. Jim had pulled back from the need to chase anyone across the rice paddies. The reality of what had happened brought us all back to the realization of where we really were: in a war zone. We decided we had been the target of a command detonated mine. Since this was at least the second time we had visited the compound, following the same route for two consecutive days this time, our movements were well known and were regular. Each morning the jeep with Americans had gone east to some location and then in the late afternoon they had returned.

There was plenty of time for the enemy to set up a mine and then wait for us to pass. The challenge for the bad guys was to detonate the mine/explosive device at precisely right time. If it was too early it would miss the target either in front of the lead vehicle or would hit the space between the two vehicles. If it was too late, it would detonate harmlessly behind the second vehicle. On our lucky day the enemy was either a little early or a little late depending on the intended target because the mine detonated almost exactly in the empty space between the two jeeps, thereby making a tremendous explosion but essentially missing both vehicles. Our being late and driving like maniacs is probably what saved us. The high speed made it more difficult to detonate the mine at the right time. Of course there is the possibility that the enemy was perfect in the execution of his plan and the distance between the vehicles was more than he expected. If we had been closer to each other his timing was right on. We had never talked about maintaining a certain distance between the vehicles. For some unknown reason we were close to the separation distance we needed to survive. The enemy was totally prepared but was unable to judge our speed which caused him to just hit the space between the jeeps.

With renewed respect for our adversary we jumped back into the jeeps and returned to our units. "Doc" Anderson had a slight concussion but that was the extent of our injuries. The second jeep lost its windshield and had a few "wounds" on its front left side.

There was no question that we had been careless. I remembered my carelessness when I had gone out to check the listening post of my US Marine platoon shortly after my arrival in Vietnam in 1967, and the time I had wandered around in the enemy base camp at night without a radio. Both times I had not been harmed and had escaped danger. I had promised myself that I would be more careful. Now I had almost been victimized by a command detonated anti-personnel device because of my own stupidity and my weakness to maintain total attention to the dangers at hand. How long would I be so lucky?

CHAPTER 9

MEDEVAC

After returning to our units from our day of fun gone bad, we were back on an operation and back into the routine. The battalion was moved by helicopter into an area with a plan to sweep along a treeline to look for suspected enemy positions and a possible base camp. The first day of the operation went smoothly with no enemy contact. The battalion, operating with its typical dual axis approach, took up positions on opposite sides of a canal and moved carefully along it. We spent the night with no mortars or other signs of the enemy.

In the morning we continued to move along the canal and encountered a number of small canals and water-filled ditches that we had to cross. At first it was just a nuisance to have to cross the little stretches of mud and water, but soon it became extremely difficult for me physically. As we continued I felt something was wrong with me. I had become extremely fit during my time in country and never had trouble keeping up with everyone else. But this day was different; something was not right.

Morning became afternoon and I was getting worse. I had severe cramps and stomach pain. The cramps would come on and deliver incredible pain to my chest and abdomen. I would have to stop and moan in discomfort. After a few minutes the pain would subside and I could move again. It seemed that the physical effort of dragging my feet over and through the wet ground was slowly wearing me out. When a cramp would hit I couldn't breathe and had to stop and bend over to deal with the pain. The time between attacks got shorter and soon I was almost constantly in a state of total paralysis in terms of being able to put one foot in front of the other. I knew about asthma attacks since I had experienced them while living in Costa Rica. This was not an asthma attack. I called Major Corah on the radio and told him I was having real problems and didn't see how I could continue. I told him I had no idea what was wrong but it was not getting better and actually getting worse. Physically I had the pain and mentally I had the uncertainty and fear of what could be wrong.

Major Corah called for a helicopter medevac. I was so ashamed and disappointed in myself. Here I was the assistant advisor with the elite VNMC and I was getting a medevac not for a wounded Marine but for me. By the time the helicopter arrived I was doubled over in pain and barely able to walk. Once aboard, I lay on the floor of the chopper and prayed that whatever was wrong could be fixed.

The helicopter took me to a US compound nearby. It was not the same place we had gone for our day of fun but was similar. It had a small medical facility which is where I went. I don't remember too much about what happened. I know I arrived at the facility and was given some very strong pain medication and put to sleep in a bed with clean, white sheets. I am not sure how long I slept or how much attention I received the rest of that day and night. I only know I woke up the next day with no pain. I was better. It was a miraculous transformation from where I had been the day before. I asked the medical personnel what had been wrong with me. No one knew. I asked if it could have been colic or something like that. They said that was a possibility but really couldn't confirm anything as having been the cause. It may have been a cumulative effect of fatigue, nerves, and stress. Once the pattern of pain started, there had been no way to stop it. But now I felt normal and knew I had to get back to work. I had some breakfast, rested comfortably and arranged to get a chopper ride back to the battalion in the afternoon.

During my absence, another advisor from the Task Force Headquarters had been flown to the battalion to take my place. As fate would have it, the battalion got into a fight that night and my replacement had an exciting time doing what was supposed to be my job. It only made me feel more embarrassed that I had to leave in the first place.

My return to the battalion went fine. Everyone was kind and happy to have me back. I was so grateful for having been lucky enough to get the medevac and medical attention I needed. Now I was back and ready to pick up where I had left off.

Shortly thereafter toward the end of March, Major Corah completed his normal tour of duty and left the battalion to rotate back to the States. When he left I asked the MAU commander what would happen to me. Since all of the other senior advisors were majors, it was most likely I would probably get a new senior advisor and remain as the assistant or junior advisor as a captain. I didn't want that to happen. I had five months as a US Marine platoon leader in the north and now had almost five months as an assistant advisor with the VNMC. I told Colonel Schaefer I preferred to be transferred to the Task Force Headquarters if I couldn't become the senior advisor. I did not want to stay in the battalion as the assistant with a new senior advisor. Since I was the junior captain among the battalion assistant advisors-- affectionately referred to as Robin the Boy Wonder--it would be hard to find someone junior to me. But there was a first lieutenant working with the Task Force Headquarters, Lieutenant Earle Hawks, who had arrived in country a few days earlier who would become my assistant and I would be the senior advisor. This change in status would now make my counterpart the battalion commander, Major Binh, which would mean that I didn't have to work directly with the XO, Captain Nhung, any more. It also meant I would be a little more out of the line of fire since the XO usually went with the lead elements while the CO moved with what served as the reserve force within the battalion.

Before I had a chance to get too comfortable, however, I was told the Second Battalion would be assigned to the Mobile Riverine Force (MRF). This meant we would be operating with the U.S. Navy and

Army in combined operations. This was one of the missions that was rotated among the Vietnamese Marine battalions. Each of the 6 VNMC battalions would get a rotating 60-day assignment to the MRF. This would give each battalion an annual opportunity to work in the riverine environment which was critical to maintaining their skills in riverine and amphibious operations. The prospects of operating with the riverine forces sounded both challenging and exciting. Our assignment with the MRF in the Delta would show me another aspect of the war in Vietnam. Just when I thought I knew so much, I was to find out I knew so little. The MRF would turn out to be a busy hectic time which would culminate in our being recalled to Saigon for the biggest battle of my tour.

CHAPTER 10

MOBILE RIVERINE FORCE

Major Corah finished his time with the battalion, completed his administrative out processing and left for his home back in the world. The battalion prepared to move to Dong Tam to join the Mobile Riverine Force (MRF). Initially I would be the lone advisor with the battalion but expected Lt. Hawks to arrive shortly. The actual assignment appealed to me for a number of reasons. First, I felt the Marines should be working near water and not just patrolling the rice paddies like normal infantry of the Vietnamese Army. Since we didn't have the opportunity for large amphibious operations, working along the rivers and canals of the Delta seemed like a worthy substitute. Secondly, working with the MRF would provide an opportunity to work with other services in combined operations. Working with the U.S. Navy and Army would mean our logistics and fire support should be good. Finally, I preferred to fight in the Delta. The enemy was forced to operate in the treelines which were along all rivers and major canals and waterways. The open rice paddies were too dangerous for him in the daylight because of our control of the air. Knowing that he had to stay in the treelines was reassuring to me. Compared to operating in the heavy vegetation of I Corps near the demilitarized zone in the north and III Corps north of

Saigon, where the enemy could be and was everywhere, I decided that I liked the Delta. The big drawback of the Delta was the difficulty of moving by foot across a terrain that was filled with rivers, canals, rice paddies and the associated mud. It looked, however, like most of that problem would be minimized when we were with the MRF because the boats of the MRF could move us on water and the helicopters of the Army could move us over the land.

We moved into the Dong Tam area in late March-early April and established a battalion position. Lt. Hawks arrived within a couple of days, leaving Task Force Bravo in Can Tho and joining the Trau Dien as the assistant advisor. He was older than I was and very experienced. He had served as an enlisted Marine in Okinawa before being selected for officer candidate school. He had attended the Military Assistance and Training Advisor Course at Ft Bragg, North Carolina before coming to Vietnam so was totally qualified for the role of advisor. I was so fortunate that the MAU had a lieutenant to be my assistant and even more fortunate that he was so prepared for the job. We met our US counterparts in the Navy and Army and prepared to start conducting tactical operations. The operational routine called for two infantry battalions to go out on most operations with one battalion being in reserve. There were two US Army battalions and our one Vietnamese Marine battalion. As noted earlier, this was a rotating 60 day assignment among the VNMC battalions so what actually happened was the Vietnamese Marine battalion went on all operations and the two Army battalions took turns, with one battalion operating and the other in reserve. This put a lot of pressure on the VNMC battalion but everyone knew the assignment would be over after two months. A typical operation lasted 1-3 days. It usually started early in the morning with a movement by boat to an objective area where we would assault/disembark and then conduct a search and destroy operation along a river or canal or across the less vegetated area between canals. When we had completed the combat search of the area, we would link up with the boats at a predetermined location and go back to the base camp. Some operations were one day in duration and involved only the Second Battalion. The tempo slowly became tiring since we were on all operations, either operating alone or with one of the US Army battalions.

Contact with the enemy was light but consistent. We invariably found something on every operation. We took a few prisoners and recovered a variety of weapons. There was no doubt that the enemy was operating in the area. There were times when we would make contact with the enemy but were unable to pursue him on foot fast enough to capture anyone. To be truly effective MRF operations required ready availability of helicopters to respond with a reaction force when the enemy was flushed from his treelines. A couple of times we had the boats and helos just when we needed them. We were able to locate, contain, and defeat the enemy easily. On one occasion the BN CO and I were in a chopper directing artillery from the air while gunships engaged the enemy in an open area. We also had elements of the battalion on the ground putting pressure on the fleeing enemy. It was an example of technology truly being effective against the less sophisticated enemy. This was in sharp contrast to when my platoon walked out of the DMZ with tanks and Ontos both of which were totally ineffective and even a liability. But flying in helicopters was not the safest thing to do. After the day's operation was over, we returned to an area to rejoin the battalion on the ground. As we were preparing to land, the engine stopped. We weren't very high in the air, maybe 50 feet, and we just floated to the ground. The helicopter rotor continued to turn, auto rotate it was called, and we dropped to the ground with a thud. We landed in a sandy area which reduced the impact. I was so thankful the engine hadn't stopped any earlier when we were much higher in the air. It was yet another close call for me with no bumps or bruises. It was also another lesson about technology having its own inherent risks. Helicopters are great assets as weapons platforms and cargo carriers but they are dangerous in terms of their falling out of the sky.

Operating with the boats wasn't always emotionally comfortable. Some of our operations found us going from big river to little river to large canal to little canal to tiny waterway. As we moved onto smaller and smaller waterways we became more vulnerable to attack from the banks. Since the majority of the vegetation was concentrated along the banks, our visibility and room to maneuver got smaller as the waterway got narrower. The boats were armored and provided reasonable protection against small arms fire but did little against the enemy's B-40 (RPGs, rocket propelled grenades) and B-41 rockets. Our boats were modified landing craft that could perform a variety of functions. We had a command boat, a boat that carried an 81mm mortar and of course boats carrying the troops. I remember how the stress level would increase as we departed a major river and started up a smaller one. In the big river we could see both banks and they were pretty far away. At least they were far enough to make us a difficult target. We would use the organic machine guns on the boats to often recon by fire. This was a tactic to shoot at the treelines along the waterways, whatever size, to see if we could draw fire from the enemy. Sometimes they returned fire and then we knew where they were. This was good for us. From their perspective it was stupid to return fire because once they did we could call in air support or artillery and hammer their position. When nothing happened with our attempts to make the enemy reveal himself, we would continue along the sequence of big to smaller to little in terms of waterways. It was like a poker game. Who would show his hand first? The early response by the enemy would give us an advantage as we moved closer to an objective.

There were times when we continued through this environment of slowly decreasing size and visibility until the vegetation from both banks would be brushing against the sides of the boats. It was terrifying to be on the boat and be so close to a possible enemy position. We really couldn't see far enough to detect any enemy forces. We could hear and feel everything and nothing. The noise of the boats was enough to cover any noise of the enemy moving along the banks. The farther we went under these conditions the more vulnerable we became to any enemy force.

If we were fired upon while en-route to an objective area we usually assaulted the enemy position. The boats would turn into the bank and the Marines would disembark straight at the enemy, hoping to fix them in place while we called in gunships or other support. Otherwise we continued on to the planned objective. The boats would continue to randomly use their 50 caliber and M-60 machine guns to recon the river banks as we moved toward an objective. We also had helicopter gunships flying along both banks of any waterway ahead of us. They looked for enemy movement and also routinely fired along the banks to see if they could draw fire from any enemy troops. The helos had the advantage of being able to see both sides of any treeline. When we were on the canal, we could only see as far as the vegetation along the banks. This practice of doing a reconnaissance by fire consumed ammunition and created noise but it resulted in the enemy revealing his position earlier than he wanted to enough of the time to make it worthwhile.

As had happened with my platoon before and now with the

battalion, I managed to have more close calls. One time, after leaving the boats, I was walking along a canal and we were taking sniper fire from our right. It wasn't close to me so I wasn't particularly concerned. But a bullet hit a branch over my head right where I had been walking seconds before. Luckily I had just bent over to look at the trail. That was the only round fired in my direction. The Marines deployed and made quick work of the sniper. During another operation we had debarked from the boats and were pursuing an enemy force on foot. The vegetation was thick along the canal and we were moving through it quickly. At one point I arrived at a small stream and came to a stop. I don't know why I stopped but I did. Just as I stopped I saw a line of splashes go across the stream in front of me where bullets were hitting the water. The splashes stopped and I continued running forward across the stream to the other side. I remember thinking the scene looked like a movie with phony splashes in the water only they weren't phony. I don't know if I had been the target or not. Again I was safe.

Another time we moved across a large open area among the rice paddies near a small collection of huts. It looked like a little hamlet but didn't really have the feel of a farming village. We could see some women walking around but no men. As we searched the area one of the Marines walked along the bank of a small canal that had various water plants growing in the water. He noticed some reeds sticking up from the surface of the water that didn't look right. I watched him just stand there and stare at the water. Then just like in the movies, he bent down and pulled the reeds out of the water and up popped some bad guys. We had stumbled onto an enemy field medical facility. The women were nurses and the men were wounded soldiers who were being treated. They had hidden in the water as soon as they saw us approaching. The South Vietnamese questioned the prisoners but didn't get many good answers. Then for the first time, the battalion became more aggressive with the prisoners. They increased the chances of getting answers to their questions by holding the enemy's head under water for a short time. It didn't have the feel of torture but rather an effort to convince the prisoners as quickly as possible that they were serious about getting some information. It all happened so fast I found it was over before I could object or suggest they stop. The prisoners quickly started talking and were then well treated. They were given food and cigarettes. Actually that was the only time I observed any rough treatment of a prisoner. The Marines were harder on their own men than they were on prisoners. I observed them tying enlisted Marines to a tree and then hitting them with a stick for various infractions. Strangely no one seemed concerned, including the punished Marine. It was almost as if everyone knew the punishment was deserved and things would be better when it was over. Clearly their system of reward and punishment was different from what I was used to, but it seemed to work. Discipline and dedication were obvious throughout the battalion.

I will never forget one operation when we encountered a small enemy force near a village. The firefight lasted only a few minutes as the Marines quickly moved into the village. The enemy took refuge in a bunker which was under one of the village huts. No one knew how many enemy soldiers were in the bunker since the people inside were silent. The Marines implored them to come out and surrender, promising that they would be taken prisoner and not harmed. Nothing happened. The enemy remained silent and refused to leave the bunker in spite of the spoken promises. While the Marines were trying to decide how best to handle a difficult and uncomfortable situation, a grenade came flying out of the bunker and exploded in front of the opening. No one was hurt but that was all that was needed to make a decision. The Marines immediately threw grenades into the bunker and then after a short wait went in and removed the enemy dead. It all happened so fast and matter-of-factly. I felt a strong sense of frustration and disappointment with what were needless deaths but didn't have a better solution. My previous need for enemy bodies was being satisfied with no problem but this time it didn't feel good. With the bunker clear, the battalion searched the rest of the village and was soon on the move again.

While working with the MRF we conducted 20 operations in the first 30 days. The fast tempo was tiring but I must admit the operations were interesting and challenging. I always felt we were close to the enemy. The intelligence was good and the support of the boats and helicopters was everything I had hoped it would be. We operated through April and into May at the same intensity. On 10 May we were alerted we would be leaving the MRF the next day and returning to Saigon. Saigon had sustained a major combined attack by VC and NVA forces on 5 May and the intelligence reports forecast another major attack on the city, similar to those of the Tet Offensive earlier in the year. The Trau Dien were needed back in Saigon. Our time with the MRF was over as was most of my tour in Vietnam. I was starting to think of returning to Pam and the States with only about one month left on my tour of duty. Funny how things happen but it would turn out that my tour would end with the largest fight of my time in Vietnam.

CHAPTER 11

Tet II

On 11 May, we went through the routine of loading the battalion onto trucks and jeeps and traveling north from Dong Tam to Saigon. It was a road trip we had made a number of times. The trip was completed without any major incidents, only a few sniper rounds as we worked our way north. Initially we were assigned the Phu Lam A sector of Cholon, the Chinese section of Saigon, on the southern end of the city. Major Binh deployed the battalion throughout our assigned area with the expectation of a major attack. We were close to an important US Army Communications Center along with a key bridge and the Phu Tho Racetrack. All three of these positions were outside our area of tactical responsibility but they represented key intermediate objectives for any enemy force. Loss of the racetrack would mean the loss of a key landing zone for our reinforcements.

For the next two weeks we patrolled our assigned area of Cholon which resulted in our officers and troops becoming very familiar with the area. This included knowing the insides of the buildings and establishing good relationships with the local residents. Things changed quickly on 25 May with a major attack on the north side of the city in the area of Gia Dinh near Tan Son Nhut airport. In response the battalion was loaded aboard trucks on 26 May and moved to Gia Dinh where we were immediately engaged in a firefight in support of the Marines of Task Force Alpha. But then Major Binh received word that the part of the defensive perimeter previously held by the battalion had not been filled in with a replacement unit. As a result, Major Binh sent Lt. Lanh and 2nd Company and asked if he could also have Lt. Hawks go with them to assist with the coordination of fire support. So off they went on the 26th with the intelligence reports now saying there would be a major attack through Cholon that same night. Meanwhile the rest of the battalion stayed at the new location and continued with its mission of clearing the buildings in the area of operations.

Lt. Hawks, Lt. Lanh and 2nd Company moved back to Cholon and took up positions as best they could to fill the empty gap. What had been held by the battalion now fell on the shoulders of a company. Lt. Lanh knew he was holding a perimeter line far greater than what was normal for a company. He checked his troops, looked at their positions and did his best to get them ready for an attack. Lt. Hawks notified the watch officer at MAU HQ of his situation and started the initial preparations for air support. He also maintained radio contact with me via the Leatherneck network. Lt Lanh did the same with Major Binh. Both Major Binh and I were uncomfortable with having one of the companies operating in the other part of the city while we stayed where we were. And as predicted, 2nd Company did in fact have a major attack precisely at midnight. Prior to the assault, their command post had been hit with RPGs, literally destroying the third floor of their building. The 2nd Company was immediately heavily engaged by elements from two battalions with enemy soldiers from both NVA and VC units. As the fighting continued, the enemy pushed abandoned vehicles into an intersection near the Marine position. They set the vehicles on fire and fueled the fire with furniture, wood, anything that would burn. Lt. Lanh asked for gunship support and Lt. Hawks quickly communicated with the MAU watch officer since he could not talk to the helos directly even though he could hear them. It was just another reality of combat and the fog of war. Lt. Hawks used the burning vehicles as a reference point for marking the friendly position and enemy targets. It should have been perfect and easy to see. Major Binh and I were powerless to do anything in the way of support.

Within a short time two gunships arrived, Razorback One and Two, and appeared to be perfectly lined up to engage the target. They passed over Lt. Hawks' position, continued toward the target and then passed by without firing. Lt. Hawks and Lt. Lanh looked at each other with total surprise and wondered why the helos hadn't fired. Lt. Hawks quickly contacted the MAU and listened to the exchange between the watch officer and the pilots. He heard the pilots say they couldn't see any burning vehicles in the intersection but were on their way for a second pass. Again the helos approached as though they were on a perfect heading and for the second time did not fire. Lt. Hawks asked the watch officer what was going on. The pilots again reported they couldn't see any burning vehicles. They could see the tracer rounds and explosions from a firefight but no vehicles. Lt. Hawks asked for one more run before the helos returned to their base at Tan Son Nhut airport. It wasn't necessary since the choppers were already on their way for a third run.

This time things were different. Lt. Hawks and Lt. Lanh made a makeshift strobe light with a laminated plastic map case and a flashlight. The pilots saw their light and finally saw the burning vehicles. Razorback One rolled in on the target and laid a devastating volume of rocket and machine gun fire around the burning vehicles and on up the street. As soon as he had completed his pass, VC and NVA troops rushed into the intersection to recover their dead and wounded and seemed to forget the fact of a second helo. Razorback Two rolled in on the target and continued the attack. The two helos made two more firing runs before returning to Tan Son Nhut. Their effectiveness cannot be overstated as they stopped all activity in the intersection.

Lt. Lanh continued to check the positions of his Marines and encourage them throughout the night. The fighting was intense and often under hand-to-hand conditions. 2nd Company made no attempt to move to new ground or pursue the enemy. They held their positions and let the enemy come to them. Eventually the enemy had taken so many casualties that he stopped assaulting and just tried to fix the battle where it was until more VC/NVA forces could arrive. In the morning of the 27th the area was littered with bodies and blood trails. The Marines were reinforced with a Vietnamese Ranger company later in the morning and the next day, the 28th, Major Binh received orders to send 1st Company from the battalion location north of the city. Later that same afternoon Major Binh and I returned to Cholon with the rest of the battalion. It was good to have everyone back together again. Lt. Lanh and his company had done a great job during their time alone but now the battalion with its full capability was back in Cholon and ready for what everyone said was another major assault.

While 2nd Company was in Cholon, we had continued to clear enemy forces south and east of Tan Son Nhut. Our encounters were brief but intense. Invariably the enemy was located in a single building. The Marines were able to isolate the building and then conduct an assault which resulted in either enemy dead or prisoners. I remember taking 8 or 9 prisoners with very little fight. Many of the enemy soldiers were young and didn't appear to be well trained or informed about the military situation in South Vietnam. It was like someone had wound them up to act like soldiers and they were doing the best they could. Our situation during the two days was nothing compared to the intensity of 2nd Company's contact in Cholon but it was enough to keep us sharp and ready. We had the battalion back together and deployed throughout our assigned area by mid afternoon which felt good to all of us.

The latest intelligence reports said the enemy presence in Cholon was much larger than initially expected and it was massing its forces and would be making a major attack against the city from that southwest direction. The battalion set up its small command post (CP) in a small two-story house which was riddled with bullets. The evidence of previous fighting was everywhere in terms of damage to the buildings. I could hear the sounds of on-going small arms and automatic weapons fire to the front. We were located on a main street about 200 meters from the major intersection where the enemy had placed the burning vehicles. The Marines had deployed forward and were on both sides of the street from our CP position to the intersection and a little beyond. The enemy had strong positions on the other side of the intersection. It was noisy, confusing and tense. At the same time there was a certain sense of calm around Major Binh and his men. It was like now that the battalion was back together they fully expected to take control of the situation and just needed some time to do it. In their minds, the end of this story was not in doubt.

As I was trying to get a better idea of where everyone was located and exactly where the enemy positions were established, I noticed two U.S. Army men near a jeep and trailer. I asked them what they were doing and they said they had been there all day waiting for a chance to recover a dead Army sergeant who was lying in the intersection. The three of them were public affairs soldiers who had been too close to the combat in the morning. One had been shot and killed and the other two had been forced to withdraw without being able to recover his body. They had spent the rest of the day looking for an opportunity to get into the intersection to get the body out but had been unable to do so. The arrival and deployment of the rest of the battalion had allowed us to take better control of the intersection and possibly could permit a recovery effort.

Most of the enemy fire seemed to be coming from their positions along both sides of the street on the other side of the intersection. I could see the body lying on the ground just short of the intersection. For some reason, I knew we could get the body and we would be ok. I have no idea why I thought this but I did. The firing continued around us but I just tuned it out. I told the two Army soldiers to get in the jeep and we would just drive as fast as we could to the intersection, pick up their dead friend, and then get back to where we were standing. They looked at me with skepticism but must have felt my confidence that we could do it. It all seemed so simple. So we did it. We got in the jeep, drove at high speed to the intersection, skidded to a stop, jumped out, loaded the dead sergeant into the trailer behind the jeep, and drove back to my position. There was a lot of shooting coming from everywhere. I have no idea if the enemy realized what we were doing and was shooting at us or if he was just engaged in the other battles going on. But I think our move was such a surprise to the enemy that we were in and out before he knew what had happened. I also told myself that most of the shooting was by the Marines of Second Battalion laying down suppressive fires to give us some cover so we could complete our short mission. The sergeant looked terrible after a day in the hot sun; already he was beginning to swell and become a haven for flies. My stomach turned as we lifted the stiff and stinking body into the trailer. Again my mind flashed ahead to my going home within a couple of weeks. The dead sergeant in my hands reminded me how quickly tragedy could strike.

The two Army men were extremely grateful for the help, thanking me for making the recovery happen before they left to return to their normal unit. One of them was a photographer and had taken pictures while the other two of us were loading the sergeant into the trailer. I wasn't aware he was taking pictures, but a few days later someone delivered a large envelope to the battalion CP with copies of the photos for me. They caused me to relive the incident yet another time.

With the body of the sergeant recovered and on its way for proper handling, I now turned my attention to what was happening with the battalion. It was getting close to dark so we decided to stay in the house serving as our CP at least for this first night. The fighting continued through the evening with sporadic fire all night. We were mortared at night and received B-40 rocket fire early in the morning.

The sounds of the rockets and mortars were greatly magnified while inside the building, reverberating and echoing off the walls. The battle raged throughout the next day, the 29th. We used tanks to attack enemy positions in the buildings. The tanks were invulnerable to the small arms fire of rifles and machine guns. They were vulnerable to rocket propelled grenades and rockets. The tanks would bring fire to a building while Marines would move in closer and then storm the building. Little by little buildings were cleared and secured.

We also had helicopter gunships providing air support with their rockets and machine guns. They could do the same thing as the tanks except from the air. The helicopters had the advantage of their speed and the long range of their weapons. But they too were at risk from enemy fire. The entire scene was surreal. We were in what had once been a normal suburb/city with narrow crowded streets, buildings, homes, some open areas and shops; all the things a little city should have. But we were fighting a serious battle with little regard for the city around us. I moved forward on the back of a tank while it fired on a cement building. I felt close to the battle because of the smells and sounds but still couldn't see any clearly defined enemy. This was similar to the major fight my platoon had experienced coming out of the demilitarized zone in July of last year: shooting going on everywhere but no real visual contact with the enemy. But this time I knew the Marines in the lead elements had visual contact and they pressed the fight. When all of this was over I knew I would see enemy dead and wounded.

Sometime during the day on 30 May, Lt. Hawks was on the roof of a building with Captain Nhung, the XO, when he was fired on by a sniper about 30 meters away. One of the rounds hit him in the front of his helmet. He remained conscious even though his face and head were covered with blood. Two Marines helped him down from the roof and into the street to get to the battalion CP. We had the battalion medical officer on site who quickly assessed the situation and stated somewhat theatrically that Lt. Hawks would live. The AK-47 round had knocked off his helmet, struck a rivet in the helmet's fiber glass liner and welded a dime-sized piece of fiberglass to his forehead. We were unable to get a medevac helo to our position so I called for a medevac vehicle which showed up in record time. He went first to the VNMC medical facility at the Navy Yard and then was moved by helo to the US Army's 3rd Field Hospital. He suffered a concussion, broken nose, and damage to his eyes. Even with these problems he returned to duty with the battalion in seven days. Sadly the long term physical and mental effects of his being shot have worsened over time.

The battle in Cholon continued for five very intense days. Little by little captured enemy equipment and weapons were brought to the battalion command post. Mortars, machine guns, rifles, pistols, and vast quantities of ammunition were neatly displayed in front of the

CP house. Major Binh presented me with one of the captured Chinese Communist pistols which I was able to get approved for bringing home with me as a war trophy. We took many prisoners during the five days and quickly sent them to other military intelligence forces for questioning. After the battle was over, we were visited by large numbers of military and media people. The battle was being referred to as Tet II or Mini Tet. When compared with the Tet Offensive of January, I guess it was a mini version. But comparing what the Second Battalion encountered in Tet I and this battle in Cholon, this was our Tet. There was nothing mini about it.

We had reported killing over 200 enemy combatants and the press visitors to the CP wanted to see the bodies. At that time during the Vietnam War there had been much printed and broadcast about inflated "body counts" by all allied forces but especially by South Vietnamese forces. Major Binh wanted to make sure the press knew his estimates were not inflated. I remember taking members of the press through the rubble of the battle and showing them piles of bodies that had been placed in mass graves. Many of the graves were makeshift combinations of pieces of sheet metal, wood, etc. all stuck in a pile with the bodies underneath in an attempt to hide them. The dead enemy bodies were young, many of them young teenagers. Those we captured and were able to question told of being promised a great victory in Saigon. They had been given weapons and ammunition and told to just attack the city and everything would be fine. But they were really not prepared to fight against a regular force in a pitched battle. They were shocked at how things actually went when they encountered the Marines and were engaged by them. That day we actually counted 223 bodies. As the press started to leave, Major Binh told them to visit the 2nd Company CP so they could see the NVA prisoners which were currently in the process of being interrogated before transfer to another location. There were 17 prisoners. Major Binh emphasized there was no inflation of enemy dead or captured by his battalion, the "Crazy Water Buffaloes."

For me it was a great victory. The Marines had done a superb job of fighting in the urban environment. The over 220 enemy dead, the captured arms and equipment, and the prisoners all added up to one great outcome for me. Finally there was something to show for our efforts and plenty of it. It was as though this one battle justified the frustrations of losing the trapped enemy in the Delta, of being mortared west of Con Thien with the platoon, and of suffering almost a year of incredible physical and emotional hardship. We had just won a major battle with minimal casualties to us, a battle that would be officially named Tet II. I was somewhat uncomfortable with my need to see bodies and count the dead but I told myself it was ok; I was just looking for results to help justify the incredible commitment so many people were making and had made.

It was now the beginning of June and time for me to start the process of returning home to the States. A Marine major, Major

Boyce Monroe, newly arrived in Vietnam, came to the battalion to take my place as senior advisor. I said goodbye to Major Binh and the other officers of the battalion with a certain amount of mixed emotions. I had placed my life in their hands for almost seven months and they had taken good care of me. Now I would go home and they would stay and continue fighting. I told myself it was their country and their duty to defend it. I had to go home to my family.

As I prepared to leave the battalion and what we called the field, I realized I had very little to pack up and transport to the BOQ room at the Splendid Hotel. My meager belongings fit inside my pack and a medium sized ammo can. I made sure my new war trophy ChiCom pistol was included with my regular stuff. I would have 10 days in Saigon to complete my administrative out processing. This included making arrangements for the shipment of my personal effects to my next duty station. I didn't expect to have any difficulties or surprises during the few days in Saigon. Again I would be wrong. The last 10 days in country still had a couple of twists to keep me on my toes. First, however, I would reflect on my year in Vietnam and look for similarities and differences between my precious days with the US Marines in I Corps and my time as an advisor with the incredible TQLC in III and IV Corps. I knew I was among a special group of people who had the experience of serving with two different organizations, including one from the host country.

CHAPTER 12

TWO WORLDS IN THE SAME WAR

I don't know how many people who served in Vietnam actually had the experience to work first with their home country military service and to then work with the sister military service of the host country. I know I was not unique and probably one of many. I had no idea when I arrived in country that I would have this experience of living under similar but also very different conditions during my tour in Vietnam.

The first difference was the length of the tour. When I arrived to serve with First Platoon of Echo Company, Second Battalion, Ninth Marines I expected to spend 13 months in country. I had a variety of calendars where I could cross off the days as I got closer to rotating home. Sometimes I would forget to mark the day because of what we were doing. Then when I had a chance to think about the passing time, I might mark off multiple days at once. That was always a good feeling. The day I was assigned to the Marine Advisory Unit, my tour length immediately changed to 12 months. This was the result of my new assignment falling under the control of MACV rather than the Marine Corps. The joy of crossing off 30 days at once was a special moment for me.

As a new platoon leader I was in charge of approximately 40 men. The actual total count was always changing as new men joined the platoon and others left, either to rotate home or because of being killed or wounded. I was responsible for their well being and responsible for operational and tactical decisions at the platoon level.

We received orders from the company and battalion levels which the platoon executed. I believed it was truly a position of incredible importance. These were my men and I had to do my best to keep them alive while trying to achieve the higher goals and objectives of senior headquarters. I worried about their families back home along with the normal issues of mail, food, water, and survival. Every day was a challenge. We lived together, fought and died together, and survived together. We were a mixture of social and ethnic backgrounds. To call us a family of fighters would be close to reality.

As an advisor I did very little actual advising. I had wondered how I would advise a group of seasoned fighters when it came to fighting the NVA and Viet Cong. Yes, I had 5 months of combat experience at the platoon level with the US Marines but did that qualify me to give advice to more senior Vietnamese officers about how to fight their war? Of course not. I quickly learned my role was to help, assist, and coordinate, not advise. I was there to help with anything that involved US forces. This meant that I could make sure all communications in English were understood by all. My focus was on making sure my Vietnamese counterparts knew what the US Forces intended to do. Then I had to make sure the Americans knew exactly what the Vietnamese wanted to happen. This was critical since the Vietnamese Marines would be using the US support to make sure they had an advantage against the enemy.

I was also there to assist with almost any request they might have. This process of providing assistance took a lot of unusual detours, like getting copies of US doctrine publications, access to US bases and their Post Exchange (PX), etc. But most importantly, I was there to coordinate the supporting arms fire that would be coming from US military forces as well as helicopter support for resupply, medevac and movement. This could mean artillery and naval gunfire support but would most likely mean support from the air. The VNMC had their own artillery that was used whenever available. If their units were out of range or otherwise not available, the US Army would help with artillery support. In my experience the best thing I did was ensure we got the best from the air support the US Air Force and Army could offer. This meant helicopter gunships, fixed wing jets and propeller driven "slow movers." I was never disappointed in terms of the aircraft providing the firepower and the forward air controllers orchestrating the delivery.

Operationally the platoon moved almost entirely by foot. There were a few instances where we moved from one area to another by truck. This usually happened at the end of an operation or the beginning of a new one. We patrolled in squad, platoon, and company sized units. We would move into a position as a battalion and then operate from that position for a few days in smaller units. I always felt we used our forces at one or two levels below what we really needed. We sent squads to do the work of a platoon, platoons to do the work of companies and so on. Most operations were search and destroy. We would move across the terrain with the hope of finding enemy forces. The advantage went to the enemy. He always was the one who initiated combat. The one exception was when we would set a night ambush. In this case we selected the location of the ambush and had control over whether or not we would trigger the ambush when the enemy forces came into the killing zone. I had the disappointing experience with the platoon when I thought everything was right but we failed to pull the trigger. This led to my later need to see bodies, living or dead from the other side.

The search and destroy missions could help to keep areas clear of enemy forces and could prevent the massing of forces for a major attack. That had been the main accomplishment of the weeks we spent patrolling back and forth along the southern edge of the DMZ. Our patrolling had kept Charlie from being able to mass enough forces for a ground attack against Con Thien. The price we paid, however, was the constant shelling from mortars, artillery, and rockets while we sat on our exposed hill south and west of the main position at Con Thien.

Most of the time I felt we were just walking around looking for trouble. At my level as a platoon leader, I didn't know enough about the intelligence reports to have a sense of how many enemy forces were actually in our area of operations. It seemed we were always a step behind, especially the time we walked to the Ben Hai River and were ambushed on the way back south. Other times we were pinned down by small enemy forces and were unable to advance without taking unacceptable casualties. When we weren't patrolling we were providing perimeter security at a permanent fire base like Cam Lo.

Operating with the VNMC was very different. First, we always moved as a battalion. As I wrote earlier, the battalion operated as two forces on a dual axis approach. This meant we had a large force all the time, nearly 800 troops. When we made contact with the enemy, this larger unit was able to maneuver quickly and react with impressive firepower. This allowed the battalion to advance and not get bogged down by a smaller enemy force. We overran the small guard post at the large base camp and also the security forces protecting the small hospital. During the long fight at the canal intersection, the battalion was able to stay engaged with the enemy force all day and into the night.

Second, the VNMC battalion often moved by helicopter, something I never did as a platoon leader with the US Marines. We used US Army helicopters to quickly move to a designated area to start an operation and at times to move to a new area in response to a

143

change in an intelligence report. Our long movement to the Mekong River Delta was by road in trucks and jeeps but once we were there we either walked, traveled in MRF boats, or flew by helicopter. I felt our tactical mobility was much higher with the VNMC than with the US Marines up north. I also felt that we had a chance of making contact on every operation. It appeared our intelligence with the VNMC was better which gave me the impression that we were going after a unit that was known rather than just walking and waiting for something to happen.

Another difference was the Marine personnel policy during the war. The USMC used an individual replacement system. This meant we went to war as individuals for our 13 month tour. This resulted in a constant state of turnover in all units; people were always leaving and people were always arriving, one at a time. Of course all people killed and wounded also required replacements which increased the rate of turnover. Coming and going as individuals influenced the level of experience in the platoon. We were always a mixture of new guys trying to figure out what to do and veterans getting ready to go home. We always said the most dangerous times in country were shortly after arrival when a new person was inexperienced and shortly before rotating home when a person tended to get careless. After the Vietnam War, the USMC changed to a unit deployment system so entire battalions now move as well trained units and deploy for a set period of time, usually 6 months.

The VNMC was totally different. The battalion was formed of young men who had been together for a long time. They were highly experienced and battle tested. Most likely they had been recruited near the home base of the battalion. The officers had years of fighting the war and were extremely proficient. The young Marines would be given time to visit their families and then they would return to the battalion. Turnover was much less when compared to the US forces. This was a clear advantage in terms of combat effectiveness.

Daily life in my Marine platoon was pretty basic. We seldom saw hot food in the field except for the C-rations (MCIs) we heated with sterno cans or heat tabs. We had a choice of 12 meals in a box. Each meal had three parts that came in a total of 4 cans. There was a meat portion, a bread portion and a desert. The food did not require water which was a great advantage. The cans, however, were heavy with each meal weighing about 2.5 pounds. We opened the cans with a P-38 can opener, usually called a John Wayne by Marines. In addition to being heavy, the cans were bulky and could make noise when we walked. Most Marines stuck some cans in their pockets and the rest in their pack. When on an extended operation we usually planned two meals per day. Sometimes we ate the food heated and other times we just ate it cold out of the can. If we were in a set position for a few days, we usually were able to combine meals to make some exotic stews. We would do the cooking in a big can that was used for fruit juices. If we were lucky we had some ground pepper or hot sauce from a care package sent from home. Having an onion was like having edible gold.

Eating as an advisor while on operation was totally different. Each evening we had a hot meal that was prepared by the cooks supporting the CO and XO. Some food was supplied through their channels and part of it was purchased from local villagers we might pass. I remember seeing the cooks walking through fields and gathering what looked like grass as soon as we would stop for the night. That grass would show up as part of the meal to mix with rice. If a village was close, someone would go get chicken, duck or pork to add to the meal. I remember one time when three or four young Marines were chasing a squealing pig all over its enclosed area trying to catch it so they could butcher it for dinner. The contest went on for a few minutes and then suddenly ended when the Marines caught the pig and quickly divided it among the cooks to be used for that night's evening meal. A couple of times I was told we had eaten dog. I found most of the food tasty and easy to eat. I had learned how to use chopsticks while traveling in Japan during one of my summers at the Naval Academy. The only negative about the food was that it wasn't quite enough for my 170 pound body and metabolism. As a result I was always on the lookout for things to supplement my diet. The obvious choice was to get some C-rats from any US unit we encountered. Other opportunities included eating in a field mess with Americans if one was close enough to visit like the time we traveled across the Delta and had been ambushed by the command detonated mine. But for the most part I did just fine on the Vietnamese diet.

With the platoon, I usually slept on the ground. We all carried an air mattress we called a "rubber bitch" or "rubber lady." They were long enough for my 6 foot frame but narrow. They required active blowing to be inflated, no self-inflating models in 1967. The mattress was heavy and somewhat bulky. It was also prone to getting a leak either from shrapnel or the many thorns growing on bushes and trees. We used two ponchos together to make a small shelter and then used the poncho liner as a blanket. Many nights we slept in the open when it wasn't raining leaving just the mosquitoes as the major distraction.

As an advisor I usually slept in a hammock. It was lightweight nylon with ropes at both ends that could be tied to trees. I erected an overhead cover with my poncho which kept the rain and dew at bay. During the night I had the radio on the ground below the hammock with the handset stuck close to my ear. I slept well in the hammock, much better than I would have imagined. It was easy to roll out of the hammock and take cover during a mortar attack. All of the Vietnamese officers slept in similar conditions as did many of the troops and non-commissioned officers.

As a platoon leader, my men and I had been dirty most of the time. Our utility uniforms were stained with sweat and often full of rips and tears. There were few opportunities to get replacement uniforms, especially trousers, so we just made do. One Marine would donate to another when necessary. We shaved out of our helmets and washed in a river or stream when we could. I do not remember ever washing any piece of clothing. We wore helmets and flak jackets all the time.

I had two sets of jungle tiger strip utility uniforms with the VNMC. My "bat boy," Private Phuc, made sure my clothes were washed regularly so I was always pretty clean. I still shaved out of a small cup. I don't remember wearing a flak jacket or a helmet. I wore a soft jungle hat like the rest of the Vietnamese officers.

Looking back made me grateful for the experience of living in these two different worlds. It made me appreciate what I had as an American and to respect the dedication and bravery of my Vietnamese Marine brothers. This experience of working with the VNMC would prove useful when I was assigned as an advisor with the Venezuelan Marines in 1975. Even though the situation would be totally different, combat vs. the peace of oil wealth, I would be able to draw on these valuable months to truly fulfill the role of an advisor.

CHAPTER 13

GOODBYE VIETNAM

I reflected on leaving the battalion. It was a fitting end to my combat tour that I would be involved in a large, significant battle that was important in the overall conduct of the war during my last days in country. The long battle in the Chinese suburb of Cholon was over and we had emerged as clear victors. I was again impressed with the tenacity of the Vietnamese Marines. They had fought extremely well, accounting for over 220 enemy dead while suffering very light casualties themselves. But now I was back in Saigon living in the luxury of a hotel room and working at the Headquarters of the Marine Advisory Unit (MAU).

Major Monroe had arrived at the battalion full of energy and enthusiasm. He was excited about the prospects of being an advisor with the "crazy water buffaloes" of the Second Battalion, Vietnamese Marine Corps. Before I actually left the battalion, we had a day together, a day of turnover, while I told him what to expect as an advisor. I had a small AM/FM transistor radio that had been valuable to me. It provided an opportunity to listen to the American radio station which was broadcast throughout Vietnam as part of the Armed Forces Radio Network with news and music. He offered to trade me a folding Buck knife for the radio. I wouldn't need the radio anymore but was sure I could use the knife so we made the trade. I already was a lover of knives and this gave me a chance to add to my small collection. The knife stayed with me for almost 15 more years before I somehow lost it while digging a ditch at my home in California. The knife had always been a reminder of the day I had physically left the battalion. When I lost it, or maybe better said when I couldn't find it, I felt as though part of me and my past were lost with it.

I had packed up my gear that last day and was driven to the Splendid Hotel. It had been months since I had seen my room or slept in my bed. The last visit had been when I returned from R&R in Hawaii with Pam at the beginning of February. It was now the first week of June, 1968. Soon I would be leaving Vietnam altogether but for now there were some administrative tasks to take care of.

First, I had to write an after action report for my total time as an advisor. This was required for all advisors before they left Vietnam. The reason was to record, for future use, the experiences and knowledge gained by all advisors both for historical reasons and to create a baseline for future advisory efforts around the world. I also had to write a "special lessons learned" about my time with the Mobile Riverine Force in the Delta. This second report with the MRF was "special" because it addressed a very important capability of Marine forces around the world, the ability to work in the riverine environment. Marines are best known for their ability to conduct amphibious operations, launching an attack from the sea against land targets using landing craft and helicopters. The riverine environment is an extension of the amphibious reality especially in an area so dominated by rivers and waterways as the Mekong River Delta. The Marine advisors working with the MRF represented a small number of Marine officers who would have first hand information about combat riverine operations which made the lessons learned so important. Both writing assignments were pleasant when compared with life in the field. I quickly adjusted to the different pace of being on my own with no real responsibilities for anyone or anything else. The MAU policy of having all advisors return to headquarters for their last 10 days in country seemed like a smart one. It provided an opportunity to start the transition from the realities of the war of Vietnam to the streets of the U.S. I remembered my transition from Vietnam to Hawaii when I went on R&R. I had truly appreciated the two days in Saigon before leaving for Hawaii. It had helped soften the shock of stepping off the plane and being in the United States. I heard stories about other officers going on R&R that went directly from the field to an airbase and then to Hawaii. Some of them were unsure if their wives would even be there when they arrived because the ability to communicate and plan was so limited. My R&R preparation and support could not have worked out better.

Now I was grateful for these few days in Saigon to again start the process of returning to a land free of combat. It was like living in a

151

half-way house after being released from prison or some form of rehabilitation. I found myself thinking more and more of the final step to really be home. Walking to and from the MAU HQ each day, enjoying time in the bar of the Splendid Hotel in the evenings, and just being free to get myself "right" must have played a significant role in my sane return to life in the US.

I had already received orders for my next assignment in the States to the Marine Barracks at "8th & I" in Washington, D.C. I wasn't really happy about the orders but considered it an honor to receive them. Marine Barracks 8th & I is the oldest active post in the Marine Corps, dating from 1801. It supports both ceremonial and security missions in the nation's capital and is home to many nationally recognized units: the Marine Corps Silent Drill Team, the Marine Drum and Bugle Corps, the Marine Band, and official Marine Corps Color Guard. I had never been overly concerned about the "spit and polish" side of the Marine Corps and the experience in Vietnam had done nothing to change my views. On the contrary, I was probably worse than before. In any event, I planned to make the most of the orders and do the best job I could.

I was allowed to ship up to 600 pounds of personal belongings as part of my permanent change of station orders from Vietnam. My main shipment of household goods would be from Carmel, CA, where Pam was living, to the next duty station in Washington, DC. It didn't take long to assemble and pack my meager personal items. I hadn't bought much of anything while in Vietnam. My stuff was mostly uniforms and some civilian clothes. I did have one new item that was special. During the spring, Captain Andrews had taken his R&R in Hong Kong. Before departing he offered to buy small items for any of the advisors who were interested in getting something special. Rolex watches were very popular at the time because of the James Bond novels with 007 wearing and using his Rolex in innovative ways. The watches were available at the China Fleet Club in Hong Kong at ridiculously low duty free prices. I took Neal up on his offer and gave him the money to get a watch. Deciding on which model to buy was tough but I finally decided on a GMT Master. It would work as a scuba diving watch with its rotating bezel and had the capability to show the time in two time zones at the same time. This somewhat extravagant purchase for me allowed me to retire the Seawolf. The Rolex is still with me today as I finish this book.

Rather than wait until the last minute, I took my household goods to the transportation office while I still had 8 days before actually leaving country and sent them on their way. This was typical of how I operated: preferring to do whatever had to be done when I could do it rather than waiting to the last minute when Murphy's Law would attack. This time, however, my being early turned out bad. As a complete surprise, two days after my boxes were on their way, my next assignment orders were changed.

A few months earlier the Marine Corps had sent out a message to all units asking for applications to the Special Education Program (SEP). I didn't apply because I felt I had only graduated from the Naval Academy in 1965, and had already spent my first two years of active duty as a student, first as a Fulbright student in Latin America and then as a student at The Basic School and Vietnamese Language School. Now in the summer of 1968 I was just completing my first real year as an infantry officer and my third year as a commissioned officer. But there was such a shortage of applicants for the SEP the Marine Corps Headquarters (HQMC) extended the deadline for applying and asked again for applicants, especially in the field of operations research.

This was the time of Secretary of Defense Robert McNamara and his team of young analysts who were referred to as the "whiz kids." Secretary McNamara had brought a new emphasis of analysis to the Department of Defense (DoD) in 1961 when he arrived from the Ford Motor Company. His approach focused on quantitative measures and forced the military services to become more modern in their management practices. The academic disciplines of operations research, systems analysis, and economic reasoning were key elements of this new focus. The military services felt that the Systems Analysis Group in McNamara's office was "doing systems analysis" to the services, like it was a punishment. The military services responded by educating large numbers of their officers in these disciplines. This is why the Marine Corps was so determined to get applicants for the SEP. One of the other advisors had applied the first time and been accepted. He encouraged me to apply and said all that could happen was that I wouldn't be accepted. So I filled out the application and mailed it to HQMC. I had also asked the Naval Academy to mail my transcripts to HQMC. I never gave it another thought. Now with just six days left before returning home, I received a set of permanent change of station orders to the Naval Postgraduate School in Monterey, California to study for a master's degree in Operations Research and Systems Analysis.

I returned to the transportation office to put a tracer on my personal goods and to have them rerouted to California. I was not optimistic about seeing my stuff any time soon. The idea of going back to school again made me change my thoughts from parades to books. I resigned myself to do whatever the Marine Corps wanted. The one great advantage of the new orders was that I would be returning to the Monterey Peninsula in California which is where I left Pam before leaving for Vietnam. We loved that part of California and going to school meant we would have over two more years there before moving on to our next assignment.

I finished my After Action Report and Lessons Learned. The ten days in Saigon passed quickly as I completed all checkout procedures. I enjoyed sleeping in my bed and eating and relaxing in the BOQ. There wasn't any combat in the city at that time which meant I was able to walk from the BOQ to the MAU Headquarters each morning and afternoon. It was like being in a normal city with no one showing any signs of concern about the war raging around them. Early one morning, with just two days to go before my departure, I was awakened by incredibly loud explosions. I rolled to the floor of my room and crawled to the door. The explosions were over almost instantly but the confusion in the hotel continued for several minutes. Almost as a parting gesture, the Splendid BOQ had been the target of an enemy rocket attack. The building was hit but suffered only minor damage. For me it was a good reminder that I was still in a country at war in spite of how things appeared walking back and forth to the MAU HQ. I had gotten careless during the past few days. The rockets helped to put me back in a state of cautious awareness.

Then it was time to go home. My bag was packed, my papers were in order, my war trophy pistol was properly registered, and my head was prepared to return to the "land of the big PX." I was driven to the airport where I went through customs and finally boarded my flight. Again there were the smiling faces of the stewardesses and all passengers. We were going home. It was amazing that these young women could change their personalities so much depending on the direction of their flight. I was one of the very few on the airplane who had seen multiple flights in and out of Vietnam. Of course I went in during June 1967. But I came out during November 1967 when I passed through Okinawa to pick up my personal gear before returning to Vietnam. It was not a commercial flight but it still had the energy of leaving South Vietnam on the way out and the reality of going back to war on the way in. I left again to join Pam on R&R in Hawaii in late January 1968, with a plane full of happy people: passengers and flight crew. Now I was leaving for what might be the last time. As the plane roared down the runway we all held our breath as though we were still within the force field of the enemy. Then the plane broke contact with the ground and a tremendous cheer erupted from every person on the plane. We cheered and hooted and cursed "Charlie" as we climbed higher and higher to safety. It was over. We had broken free. We were out of *'Nam, the 'Nam, in country,* and going back to *the world, home,* etc. Goodbye Vietnam, hello U.S.A.

CHAPTER 14

HOME

My last days in Saigon had passed very quickly. The administrative requirements of checking out of the Marine Advisory Unit (MAU) plus the writing of my after action reports had made the time fly. The actual waking up on the last day and the movement to the airport for final processing are a blur. I can't remember any details about leaving Vietnam except for the plane's actual departure. The entire plane was wild with excitement as we lifted off the ground.

The plane ride home is also a blur. Everyone settled down as soon as we had reached cruising altitude. I wasn't traveling with any friends so I didn't have a conversation partner for the trip. I did have time to reflect on the year in Vietnam but really wasn't sure what it meant or would mean. I considered myself to have been fortunate to serve both as a platoon leader with the U.S Marines and as an advisor with the Vietnamese Marines. The two different assignments had allowed me to see a large part of the country and to operate under a variety of tactical situations. The fact that I was returning home without any physical injuries or known emotional problems was also a real plus.

When I had left Pam a year ago and again after R&R, she had said she would accept me any way I came home, just so I came home. She said that she could accept physical injury as long as I had my mind. It was easy to say that you would accept something if you never really had to do it. I was coming home without a scratch. There had been plenty of opportunities for me to get hurt or killed. Somehow I had been spared. That is the only word for it because I knew how many times I had been careless and how many times I could have easily been killed. So there must have been a plan for me that went beyond Vietnam.

The plane landed and refueled someplace but I don't remember where. It may have been Hawaii or Guam. We just stopped, got fuel, and quickly returned to the air. Our destination was Travis, AFB, in northern California. Pam would meet me there with a new Jaguar sedan she had purchased a few months earlier. We had made the arrangements to get the car before I left and she had taken delivery early because Jaguar did not produce the model we wanted in 1968. As a result she got a new 1967 in early spring and had been able to use it for the previous few months.

It is a sad reality but I had worried about her having the new car while I was away. Even with the war all around me I found time to worry about a new car and how it was being taken care of. The old car was a white 1965 Olds Cutlass convertible that I named White Fang. It had been my first car which I purchased in my senior year at the Naval Academy. Like many young men felt at that time, my car was more important than it should have been. After graduating from the academy and receiving the Fulbright Scholarship to Costa Rica I faced the question of what to do with the car while I was gone to Central America. It was just taken for granted that I would fly from Washington, DC to San Jose, Costa Rica.

While I was trying to decide how to get the car home to Portville, NY for storage and then my travel back to DC, someone suggested I drive to Costa Rica. I was told there was a road all the way and most of it was paved. I asked HQMC if that would be possible and they said they would reimburse me up to the costs associated with travel by air and would allow me a maximum of 10 days of travel time if I preferred to drive. This sounded great to me. I would be able to visit relatives in Texas en route to Costa Rica. So off I went alone to drive to San Jose, easily making the trip in the assigned time including a few days in Dallas with my cousins. During the assignment in Costa Rica I took advantage of the summer break from the university and hitchhiked throughout South America which is where I met Pam. I left the Cutlass in San Jose. Then after the Fulbright was over in June, 1966, Pam joined me in Costa Rica for a few days and then we traveled back to the States together. After graduating from TBS in January, 1967, we made a trip to Mexico on our way to language school in Monterey, CA. During that trip we had a minor accident when we hit a patch of black ice in Tennessee. We did a spinout and ended up with the front of the car suspended on a guard rail. I got out of the car and hurried to the front to assess the damage. Then there was a little voice behind me saying, "I'm ok honey." That stopped me in my tracks. Pam had just reminded me that there were other things more important than the condition of the car. In all I put 50,000 miles on the car in the first two years I owned it. Pam was part of many of those miles and she knew how I felt about cars. She had completed the transaction to sell White Fang and buy the new Jaguar. Now it was June 1968, and time to see Pam and the new car.

As our plane neared the States, I thought about what life would be like back in the world. We would have hamburgers, fries, beds, sheets, cars, families, and everything else that went with "normal" living. I had read a little about the protests and demonstrations but really had been insulated from most of the negative news. During language school before I left for Vietnam, Pam and I went to San Francisco every weekend of the 11 week course. We saw the activity in the Haight Asbury section of the city and knew how many people felt about the war. At least I knew better than to expect a hero's welcome. Still I recognized that Vietnam was not a popular war and that its participants were not viewed as having done something noble. I chose not to worry about it.

We were suddenly in our final approach. As we quickly lost altitude I realized that an important chapter in my life was about to end. I was coming home after a year of combat. For sure there had been many changes in me but I wasn't sure what they were. I suspected I would start finding out very soon.

The plane came to a stop in front of the terminal. We disembarked, went through customs, and then were free. Pam was there looking great. I had been worried about what it would be like to be with her again. R&R had only been a few days. Now I was home for good. We hugged and kissed and thanked God for letting me come back. But then a feeling came over me. Some would say it was my practical nature taking charge. Others might suggest I was unable to just stop and relax. Regardless an internal voice quietly said, "That's enough; time to get in the car and go home. You have a four-hour trip ahead of you. And don't forget, the war isn't over. You will go back."

I can't explain why I couldn't truly enjoy the reality of my return. As I think back on those moments, I wonder why Pam and I didn't just sit down and relax. We could have driven to a motel, gone out to dinner, and just enjoyed being together again. But we didn't. Somehow that practical, serious side of my nature hadn't changed at all. We got in the car and drove the four hours south to Carmel. And that was just the beginning of a whirlwind four weeks.

I was happy to be home but I wasn't able to let myself fully enjoy it. First, there was the knowledge that I was only back temporarily. I sincerely believed that I would be back in Vietnam in two years. Second, there was a lot to do before I could start my classes at the

Naval Postgraduate School. The combination kept me serious, focused and tense.

Pam and I wanted to start a family which meant we needed to find a place with more room. She had lived in a small cottage while I was in Vietnam. It had worked great while I attended the Defense Language Institute before Vietnam and it had been perfect for Pam to share with her high school friend who came to live with her while both of their husbands were away. But the cottage wasn't big enough for a baby. Besides, the landlord had already rented the cottage to someone else when he knew we would be leaving. My change in orders at the last minute meant we needed to find a place immediately. Actually we needed to find another house to rent and to move our household goods within a few days because we wanted to drive across the country to visit all of the relatives before I started school in late summer. We were lucky. We found a small, two bedroom house in Carmel, signed a lease, got special treatment from the transportation people at the Navy School, moved our household goods, and headed east on our road trip all within four days. We left the house full of boxes which we would unpack after our trip. We had managed to accomplish so much in such a short time. Now I believe that this was one of the changes that had occurred in Vietnam. I truly believed that nothing was impossible. I could not take no for an answer and believed there was always a way to solve any problem. When told that there were no houses available in the

Carmel market, I said we would find one. We devoured the housing ads for rentals in the local paper and found a house we loved. When told we needed at least two weeks to arrange a move of our household goods, I said there was a way to do it within days. Working with the folks at NPS who understood our situation, we were able to arrange to have our household goods packed up at the cottage and moved to the new location in the same day. Now just four days later we were making a three-week round-trip to Portville, New York with stops in Utah, Minnesota, and Tennessee.

We drove east through Utah to see my grandparents in Provo, slept on the ground with no tent and one sleeping bag and a blanket in Yellowstone National Park, and visited Pam's family in Minnesota. It was during the time we were with relatives that I realized I didn't want to talk about the war. Even more interesting, I sensed no one really wanted to know about the war. I had gone away but now was back. When asked how it was, I would be brief and not say much. No one pushed me to explain more. They seemed happy to let the subject drop. Some people would make stupid comments or ask stupid questions about widespread drug use, atrocities, prostitutes, burning huts etc. It seems all of the negative isolated incidents that had been reported in the press were viewed as being commonplace throughout Vietnam. When I said that I had observed no drug use other than beer, they looked at me like I was either lying or hadn't really been in Vietnam. The final result was that all conversations about the war were shallow, very short and usually quickly shifted to something more interesting to the people present. I made no attempt to make people talk about the war. I made no attempt to demand understanding about what I had experienced. I was content to just let the discussion move to something else.

We completed our visit with Pam's family and drove north through Minnesota to the Canadian border. Our plan had been to cross into Canada and then drive east to Niagara Falls, Canada where we would cross back into the States. My hometown of Portville, New York was only 90 miles south of the falls, almost on the Pennsylvania border. When we arrived at the Canadian border the border people asked if we had any weapons. I had my war trophy pistol with all of the official papers which validated its capture in Vietnam and legal import into the US. The problem was that we were trying to enter Canada. I was told I would have to leave the pistol at the border; that no firearms of any kind were allowed to be brought into Canada. My official papers made no difference nor did my arguing about how the pistol was a spoil of war. I found a problem I couldn't fix the way I wanted to. Since it was not feasible to leave the ChiCom pistol at the border, we changed our travel plans and drove back to Minnesota and then east through Michigan and on to New York. We drove nonstop all the way which was unnecessary. Why did we do it? It saved time and money.

We arrived in Portville, finding the same guarded interest in the war. I had a close friend, really a "non-blood brother," a fellow member of a small group of high school friends who were known as the Vikings. He had been a Marine platoon leader for almost his entire tour. We had gone through TBS in successive classes. He was one class ahead of me. We overlapped for a few months which meant he was available to be my barber during TBS before he graduated. Now that I was home we talked a little about the war but not much. We preferred to talk about high school and the old football days. It was almost as though we didn't really want to know what each other had experienced.

After I had been home a couple of days, I received a call from HQMC. It was my assignment monitor. For every officer rank in the Marines, there is someone who is responsible for managing future assignments. My monitor told me there now wasn't enough room for me at NPS. I would have to go somewhere else for a year and then could enter the school the following year. I told him I had signed a lease on a new rental house and had already used my allowed PCS household move. He offered me Marine positions in Inspector and Instructor (I&I) duty in St. Louis, Pittsburgh, and a third "garden spot" I can't remember. The I&I duty possibilities meant I would be working with the Marine Corps Reserve. I said I wanted to go to NPS and was not interested in a one year assignment to wait for room at the school. I thought no matter what, I would have to return to California to pack up my household goods and then have them

166

shipped to the next location which would mean another costly move for the Marine Corps. He said he would call back in a day or so. After he hung up I thought about the order changes. First, I had been told I would go to 8th and I, the premier post of the Marine Corps in terms of public image. Then the orders were changed to the Navy School, and now as a stop gap to fill in a year, I was offered I&I duty at different locations. Something made me decide to fight even harder for what I wanted. When the monitor called back I made it clear I was on leave on the east coast, and was on my way back to California. I was driving back regardless of what he said and if the Marine Corps wanted to pay for another PCS household move it could do so once I was back with my possessions. I think my connection to my precious belongings had gotten stronger when I had nothing in Vietnam. He said he would call back. His next call was the last. I was told to report to the Navy School and take my chances. It turned out there was plenty of room for another Marine student at the school. The senior Marine welcomed me with open arms. Obviously the monitor had been trying to solve another personnel assignment problem and I was viewed as the easy solution. Why I resisted the monitor as such a junior officer, I don't know. Maybe it was another change from the Vietnam experience.

Pam and I completed our trip and returned to California. I quickly got into the demands of the masters program which forced Vietnam out of my consciousness. There were a number of Marines in the operations research curriculum and most of us had just returned from the war. We spent time together but most of it was studying for exams or playing rugby. We all expected to return to Vietnam after school was over so we didn't talk about the "rightness" or "wrongness" of the war. It was something we had done and would probably have to do again. That thought prevented me from honestly analyzing what was going on in Vietnam and my participation in it.

School passed quickly. The two years were over almost before I had time to appreciate the family time and the opportunity to get an advanced degree. As expected I received orders to Vietnam for a second tour. I graduated in October 1970 and set off on another cross-country trip, this time to say goodbye to the relatives. We returned to the west coast in November, checking in to Camp Pendleton where I was placed in charge of a replacement unit in what was called the staging battalion. I would be at Pendleton for three weeks while the unit went through some refresher training and completed all processing for movement to Vietnam. I left Pam with friends in San Diego when I was in the field, and had her with me at the Hostess House when I was able to be with her at night. Our family had grown to three with the arrival of a son, Dane, in March 1969 so she had a 20-month old to care for.

Finally my training in the staging unit was completed and it was time to leave. Again the pain of the upcoming separation was there. I didn't know what my job would be in Vietnam but I knew about

168

Vietnam. This time I wasn't the idealistic young warrior off to fight a war. I was a professional Marine who was going to war to do his job. If I wanted to be against the war then I could resign my commission. Otherwise, I would serve my time like everyone else. But the day before my departure, at almost the last minute, my orders were changed. It turned out the Marine Corps was already in the process of withdrawing from Vietnam. The decision was made that it would not make sense to send me to Vietnam only to pull me out within a couple of months. As a result, I would not go to Vietnam. I would instead stop in Okinawa and remain with the Third Marine Division for my 12 month tour.

So the emotional roller coaster that Pam, Dane, and I had been on for the last few months took another dramatic dip. We would still be separated but I wouldn't return to combat. I had spent so much time preparing myself mentally for the return to Vietnam that I was not sure how to react to the new orders. I was relieved, disappointed, angry, and many other things all at the same time. I thought back to how I had wrestled with my memories of the war as I tried to get ready again, and how much the war had affected the tension level within the family. Now I wasn't going.

I went to Okinawa in a daze. I saw firsthand results as the Marines were already being withdrawn from Vietnam again explaining why I didn't go. The ironic part of this story is that the officer who had encouraged me to apply for the SEP at NPS was initially assigned to

Okinawa. When he got there he was able to get his orders changed to Vietnam by switching orders with another person who had still not completed the replacement training at Camp Pendleton. It turned out I was the other officer. Later in my career I would serve as his executive officer when he commanded the Second Battalion, Fifth Marines. So I spent my second year of overseas deployment with First Battalion, Fourth Marines as a rifle company commander. When I returned home from an overseas deployment for the second time in November 1971, I was truly home. Vietnam was almost officially over with talks of ending the war in full swing. Now I could begin to think about life without the war; I could face my feelings and experiences head on rather than keep them hidden because of the expectation of having to go back. I still didn't talk much about the war nor did I suffer from it in any serious medical way. I know I was changed by the war but I prefer to think of the changes as being positive. I moved on through life completing a 20-year career in the Marines in 1985. Vietnam had been a period of growth and challenge. It was just one year of my life that I couldn't forget.

Then in 1985 I wrote down the story about checking the listening post (LP). It was a memory I couldn't forget. The young Marine who lost his eye and how close I had come to being killed made the memory a vivid one. I sent the story to the MARINE CORPS GAZETTE to see if there was any interest. The magazine liked the story and asked if I could write more. Eventually I covered my year with 17 short articles that were published in 1985-1986. After finishing the articles I tried to build them into a book but never got it done. In 2014 Pam started self publishing some children's books which reignited my desire to write my book. She encouraged me to get it done and offered to help.

I published Vietnam Memoirs Part 1: My Experiences as a Marine Platoon Leader in February, 2015. In both Part 1 and Part 2, I have tried to relive key experiences and face some painful memories. I have tried to write from the perspective of a young, idealistic Marine officer who had to accept a long separation from his new bride. I wanted to write something that could be read and valued by almost anyone. I have intentionally tried to focus on the key details of all experiences in this book. I have not tried to fill the pages with details of combat or emotional challenges of R&R. There are no details about the night of reconciliation after dinner at Duke Kahanamoku's and there are no additional details about the names of the streets and press reporters in Cholon. This was never intended to be a set of books to serve as a historical account of the Vietnam War. Rather it is the best I can do to tell my story. Sadly, I still cannot face the political reality of our losing the war.

THE UNITED STATES OF AMERICA
THIS IS TO CERTIFY THAT
THE PRESIDENT OF THE UNITED STATES OF AMERICA
HAS AWARDED THE

SILVER STAR MEDAL

TO

CAPTAIN DONALD E. BONSPER, UNITED STATES MARINE CORPS

FOR

GALLANTRY IN ACTION

ON 9 JANUARY 1968

GIVEN THIS 18TH DAY OF NOV 19 68

SECRETARY OF THE NAVY

The President of the United States takes pleasure in presenting the Silver Star Medal to

Captain Donald Edward BONSPER
United States Marine Corps

for service as set forth in the following:

CITATION

"For conspicuous gallantry and intrepidity in action while serving in the Republic of Vietnam on 9 January 1968. As Assistant Battalion Advisor to the Second Vietnamese Marine Battalion during Operation SONG THAN 810, Dinh Tuong Province, Captain BONSPER was with the lead helicopter assault companies. Captain BONSPER, with two companies, engaged in a sharp encounter with the Viet Cong 261B Main Force Battalion. Unhesitatingly Captain BONSPER moved to exposed forward positions from which he skillfully directed and controlled U. S. helicopter gunships against the enemy. The battle raged for approximately seven hours against the well camouflaged, entrenched enemy. After prolonged engagement in close contact with the enemy force, the unit expended nearly all of its ammunition. Captain BONSPER called for a resupply of ammunition for his beleaguered unit. Stationing himself in the only available helicopter landing site, which was an open field between his unit and the enemy, Captain BONSPER courageously, and in plain view of the enemy, directed the gunships and Marines' suppressive fires in an attempt to bring in an ammunition-laden helicopter. One of the gunships was hit and the resupply attempt was abandoned. In one hour, as darkness fell, another attempt to resupply the Marines was made. Once more Captain BONSPER moved from a covered position without regard for his own personal safety into the fire swept landing zone, using his unshielded flashlight as a guiding beacon. The Viet Cong immediately concentrated their fires on this light, however Captain BONSPER remained in the exposed position directing the resupply helicopter into the landing zone and at the same time, directing the suppressive fires of the supporting gunships. Upon discharge of the desperately needed cargo, Captain BONSPER directed and supervised the evacuation of the seriously wounded aboard the same helicopter. Captain BONSPER's unit, upon replenishment of ammunition, subsequently succeeded in driving the numerically superior enemy from the field of battle. His indomitable spirit, courage in the face of the extreme personal danger and superior professionalism were in keeping with the highest traditions of the United States Naval Service."

For the President

JOHN J. HYLAND
Admiral, U. S. Navy
Commander in Chief U. S. Pacific Fleet

THE UNITED STATES OF AMERICA
THIS IS TO CERTIFY THAT
THE PRESIDENT OF THE UNITED STATES OF AMERICA
HAS AWARDED THE

BRONZE STAR MEDAL

TO

CAPTAIN DONALD E. BONSPER, UNITED STATES MARINE CORPS

FOR

MERITORIOUS SERVICE FROM 20 NOVEMBER 1967 TO 16 JUNE 1968

GIVEN THIS 27TH DAY OF NOV 19 68

Paul R. Ignatius
SECRETARY OF THE NAVY

174

COMMANDER IN CHIEF
UNITED STATES PACIFIC FLEET

The President of the United States takes pleasure in presenting the
Bronze Star Medal to

Captain Donald E. BONSPER
United States Marine Corps

for service as set forth in the following:

<u>CITATION</u>

"For heroic achievement in connection with operations against the enemy
while serving in the Republic of Vietnam from 20 November 1967 to 16
June 1968. As Senior Marine Advisor to the Second Battalion, Vietnamese
Marine Corps, Captain BONSPER provided advice and assistance in coordinat-
ing and directing artillery fire support, helicopter gunships, tactical
aircraft, resupply missions, and medical helicopter support during numerous
battalion size or larger, search and destroy/security operations which resulted in many Viet Cong killed, wounded or captured. Captain BONSPER was
often subjected to direct enemy fire while participating in combat operations, and his actions were instrumental to the success of friendly forces
while engaging the enemy. Captain BONSPER's outstanding performance of
duty significantly contributed to the operational effectiveness and capabil-
ities of the Second Battalion, Vietnamese Marine Corps. His devotion to
duty, courage under fire and sense of responsibility were in keeping with
the highest traditions of the United States Naval Service."

Captain BONSPER is authorized to wear the Combat "V".

For the President

John J. Hyland

JOHN J. HYLAND
Admiral, U. S. Navy
Commander in Chief U. S. Pacific Fleet

175

GLOSSARY OF ABBREVIATIONS AND TERMS

Battalion: The basic tactical unit of the division. In 1967 the USMC battalion contained four lettered (A,B,C,D) rifle companies and the headquarters company. A VNMC battalion contained four numbered (1,2,3,4) rifle companies and the headquarters company.

B-40/41 Rocket: A variant of the RPG-2, the first rocket-propelled grenade launcher designed in the Soviet Union. The RPG-2 was a shoulder-fired anti-tank weapon designed and mass-produced in the Soviet Union and distributed to its allies. It was also produced under license by other countries, including China and North Vietnam. It was widely used against the US Military in the Vietnam War. The Vietnamese variants were called the B-40 (bazooka 40mm) and B-50.

Charlie/Charley: Term used to describe the Viet Cong, the indigenous enemy force of South Vietnam. This is in contrast to the North Vietnamese Army regulars who came as reinforcements from the north.

Company (USMC): A total of 6 officers and 176 men. This included three rifle platoons, a weapons platoon and the company headquarters. The weapons platoon had three sections: 60mm mortars, M-60 machine guns, and 3.5" rocket launchers. Each section had three squads. Usually these squads, except for the mortars, were attached to the three rifle platoons in the company. So each rifle platoon had a squad of machine guns and 3.5" rocket launchers. The company commander retained control of the 60 mm mortars.

Co Van: Vietnamese for advisor.

C-Rats: The real name as of 1958 was MCI for meal, combat, individual but most people continued to refer to them as c-rats or c-rations. The MCI consisted of a rectangular cardboard carton containing 1 small flat can, 1 large can, and two small cans. It consisted of an "M" – unit can (meat-based entree item), a "B" – unit (bread item) composed of the Crackers and Candy Can and the flat Spread Can, and a "D"-unit can (dessert item). The M-1, M-3, B-1, B-2, D-2, and D-3 unit cans were small and the M-2, B-3, and D-1 unit cans were large. The ration cans were packed upright, with the flat Spread can over the large can on the left side and the two small cans were stacked one over the other on the right side (the lighter one over the heavier one). On top were the brown foil Accessory Pack and a plastic spoon wrapped in clear plastic. There

177

were twelve different meals. The ration boxes were shipped in a rectangular cardboard packing case. Each packing case contained 12 ration cartons (containing one of each meal) packed in 2 rows of 6 rations. They were grouped in 3 menus of 4 meals each, organized by their "B"-unit (B-1, B-2, & B-3). It also contained 4 paper-wrapped P-38 can openers to open the cans. Marines referred to the P-38 as a "John Wayne."

CTZ: Combat tactical zone. South Vietnam was divided into four CTZs. They were named I through IV and were referred to as Corps. They went from north to south with I Corps in the north part of the country next to the DMZ and IV Corps in the south in the Mekong Delta.

Dai Uy: Vietnamese for the rank of captain.

DMZ: Demilitarized zone; a dividing strip between North and South Vietnam that was established in 1954. It was more than 100 kilometers long running east and west and about 2 kilometers deep. The dividing line generally followed the Ben Hai River for most of its length.

Enemy: Usually referred to with a masculine pronoun: he, him or his. It is a generic term and can mean one soldier or a large enemy force.

Firefight: An engagement between two forces involving the shooting of weapons, usually small arms of rifles and machine guns.

Incoming: A term used to describe a situation when a unit is receiving fire from an enemy force. There can be incoming fire from small arms and machine guns. This is called direct fire. No one has to call "incoming" in this situation since everyone can hear the weapons fire and the bullets going over their heads or hitting around them. In the case of artillery and mortars, the fire is called indirect since it is first fired up in the air and then the rounds come down and explode on impact with the ground. Since the source of the fire is some distance away it is hard to hear when the weapons actually fire. Artillery makes a pop or muffled blast when it fires. Mortars make a "toonk" sound when the mortar round hits the bottom of the mortar tube. Both artillery and mortar rounds take time as they travel toward the target. If someone hears the pop or toonk, he screams "incoming" to let the rest of the unit know that danger is in the air.

I&I: Inspector and Instructor. Billets within the Marine Corps to work with reserve units around the country with an emphasis on training.

LZ: Abbreviation of helicopter landing zone.

MACV: Military Assistance Command Vietnam.

MAU: Marine Advisory Unit, part of MACV.

MRF: Mobile Riverine Force. In the Vietnam War, the MRF was a joint US Army and US Navy force that comprised a substantial part of the brown water navy. It was modeled after lessons learned by the French experience in the First Indochina War and had the task of both transport (of soldiers and equipment) and combat. The primary base was at Dong Tam Base Camp, with a floating base at the base of the Mekong River. The MRF played a key role in the Tet Offensive. The Vietnamese Marine battalions operated with the MRF on a rotating basis.

NCO: Non-commissioned officer within the enlisted ranks. Corporals and sergeants were called junior NCOs and staff sergeants and above were called staff/senior NCOs.

NPS: Naval Postgraduate School. The premier post graduate institution of the US Navy and Department of Defense located in Monterey, CA.

NVA: North Vietnamese Army.

Ontos: An anti-tank, tracked vehicle with six 106mm recoilless rifles mounted on the outside of an armored hull. It had a crew of three and required someone to get out of the vehicle in order to reload the rifles.

Platoon: A total of 42 enlisted men and one officer with three squads (13 each) plus a radio operator, platoon guide, platoon sergeant and lieutenant as platoon leader.

Poncho: A rubberized piece of equipment like a blanket with a hole and hood in the center. It could be worn over a pack and other clothing for protection against the rain. Because of its rubberized surface, it did not breathe and thus caused a lot of sweating. In some cases the sweat was worse than the rain. It could also be connected to trees to provide a shelter/roof over a hammock. Two people could hook their ponchos together to make a ground shelter. Using two ponchos was better than using the intended shelter halves which were too heavy to carry by the infantry.

Poncho liner: A lightweight insulated, quilted blanket that could be tied to a poncho liner to provide added warmth. Most of the time the poncho liner was used like a blanket while sleeping on an air mattress.

PX: Post Exchange, similar to a civilian department store that provided commonly used goods for Marine families on most military bases; called a Base Exchange or BX within the Air Force.

Squad: Usually a total of 13 men with three fire teams of 4 men each plus a sergeant or corporal as squad leader.

The Basic School (TBS): The Basic School is where all newly commissioned and appointed (for warrant officers) USMC officers are taught the basics of being an officer of Marines. TBS Officer Basic Course currently lasts 28 weeks (it lasted 21 weeks in 1967), during which new officers are given classroom, field, and practical application training on weapons, tactics, leadership and protocol. Candidates are commissioned from a variety of sources, including the Naval Academy, NROTC Programs at colleges and universities, the Officer Candidates School, and Platoon Leader's Course. During TBS, the officers are selected for a Military Occupational Specialty (MOS), including, infantry, artillery, military police and naval aviator. Following TBS, the officers will attend one or more additional schools to be trained in their specialty and then assigned to a unit in the Fleet Marine Force. The

Basic School is at Camp Barrett, Quantico, Virginia. Each year over 1,700 new officers are trained.

TQLC: Thuy Quan Luc Chien, Vietnamese for Vietnamese Marine Corps.

Tracer rounds: Tracer ammunition (tracers) are bullets that are built with a small pyrotechnic charge in their base. Ignited by the burning powder, the pyrotechnic composition burns very brightly, making the projectile trajectory visible to the naked eye. This enables the shooter to make aiming corrections without observing the impact of the rounds fired and without using the sights of the weapon. When used, tracers are usually loaded as every fifth round in machine gun belts, referred to as four-to-one tracers. They are especially visible at night.

Vietcong/VC: The Communist-led army and guerrilla force in South Vietnam that fought against the government and was supported by North Vietnam. See Charlie.

VNMC: Vietnamese Marine Corps.

Whiz Kids: "Whiz Kids" was a name given to a group of experts from Rand Corporation who worked with Robert McNamara in order to turn around the management of the U.S. Department of

Defense (DoD) in the 1960s. The purpose was to shape a modern defense strategy in the Nuclear Age by bringing in economic analysis, operations research, game theory, computing, as well as implementing modern management systems to manage the huge dimension of operations of the DoD with methods such as the Planning, Programming, and Budgeting System (PPBS). They were called the Whiz Kids after the group at Ford Motor Company that included McNamara a decade earlier.

Acknowledgements

This second book about my tour of duty in Vietnam covers my experiences as an advisor with the elite Vietnamese Marine Corps. As I did in Vietnam Memoirs: Part 1, I have not used the real names of the American officers of the Military Advisory Unit or the officers and men of the Second Battalion, VNMC in order to avoid any connection to the real people. I am truly indebted to the fine men of both organizations. They both contributed greatly to my development as a young Marine officer and eventual advisor with the Venezuelan Marine Corps, 1975-1978, and infantry battalion commander of the Second Battalion, Fifth Marines at Camp Pendleton, California in 1981-82. This book is also based on the same series of articles that appeared in the Marine Corps Gazette in 1986. The Gazette owns the copyright for the articles and has given permission for their use in this book. Finally, I must express my sincerest gratitude to my wife, Pam, for her unfailing support and belief in both of my books. Without her assistance, the writing of future books would have remained a nice topic of conversation at cocktail parties. Because of her encouragement the books are now finished and available to anyone interested in the Vietnam War.